The Lure of the Big Game
A Treatise on Tennis
By Vince Ng

Published by:
Today Publishing
Suite 5
8481 Fox Hollow Dr.
Broadview Hts, OH 44147

All rights reserved. No part of this book may be reproduced or transmitted in any form or by any means, electronic or mechanical, including photocopying, recording or by any information storage and retrieval system, without written permission from the author, except for the inclusion of brief quotations in a review.

Unattributed quotations are by Vince Ng

Copyright © 2004, 2005 by Vince Ng

ISBN, print ed.   0-9765415-0-5

Printed in the United States of America

Library of Congress Cataloging-in-Publication Data

Ng, Vince

(PCN Number)
Library Congress Control Number: 2005905563

Dedicated to Olivia

What players are saying about this book:

"Competitive tennis – Exposed! ...Finally, a book that clarifies all the gray areas from a player's point of view."

"The Lure of the Big Game says what needs to be said. All the other tennis books simply beat around the bush."

"An essential book for the serious player."

"This book puts into words what separates winners from losers in competitive tennis."

"If you want to know what it really takes to win, I recommend this book."

"Better than any other tennis book out there...and definitely more interesting."

"A very worthwhile read...I'll definitely incorporate it into my approach on teaching."

"Very insightful...a look at the nature of competitive tennis, a completely different creature than tennis itself."

"I couldn't agree more with the Lure of the Big Game. I can name half the junior players who should be reading this book. This is going to be the first book on my players' reading list."

"Entertaining...and plenty of good humor. Tennis for the 21st Century."

"Thought provoking. Read carefully...not a blatantly obvious book."

"Priceless lessons from one player to another."

The Lure of the Big Game

A Treatise on Tennis

Vince Ng

**Second Edition
Revised**

℞ Today Publishing • Broadview Hts, Ohio

Contents

Foreword
Introduction
Warning – Disclaimer

1.	Finding the Will to Win	11
2.	It's Time!	13
3.	Man of Infinite Focus	17
4.	Understanding What You're Up Against	19
5.	The True Champion	24
6.	Trashtalking	28
7.	The Crosscourt Figure-8 Play	30
8.	Troubleshooting the Figure-8 Play	34
9.	Variations: Holding the Inside-Out Forehand	36
10.	Variations: Sneaking the Forehand Down the Line	38
11.	A Note about Hitting Balls at the Peak	39
12.	Using the Figure-8 Play for Defense	40
13.	Neutralizing a Big Weapon	43
14.	Two Defensive Shots to Consider	44
15.	Effective Passing Shots	46
16.	Holding Serve with a Plan	48
17.	Returning Serve	53
18.	Opportunities in Holding and Breaking Serve	56
19.	The Backhand Principle	58
20.	The Forehand Principle	61
21.	Hitting Drop Shots	63
22.	Handling Drop Shots	65
23.	The Volley Principles	66
24.	Simple Principles for Winning Doubles	69
25.	Sticking to the Plan	74
26.	Opponent Styles: The Big Server	76
27.	Opponent Styles: The Netrusher	78
28.	Opponent Styles: The Pusher	79
29.	Opponent Styles: The Counterpuncher	80
30.	Opponent Styles: The Lefty	81
31.	Stop Choking	83
32.	Strange Birds	85
33.	Enter the Zone	90
34.	The World of Cheating	92
35.	In Front of Crowds	95
36.	The Lure of the Big Game	96
37.	The Evolutionary Way of Learning	100
38.	Troubleshooting Your Progress: Find, Don't Seek	105
39.	Lost Strokes	108
40.	Keys to Junior Tennis	111
41.	Finding a Coach	116

42.	Cults	124
43.	Drills	128
44.	Before Your Kid Starts Tennis	132
45.	Stopping By Woods	136
46.	Be Your Own Man	137
47.	Tennis as a Teacher	139
48.	At the End of the Day	141
49.	Averting Tennis Injuries: Cramps	143
50.	Averting Tennis Injuries: Ankles, Shins, Behind the Knee	146
51.	Averting Tennis Injuries: Elbow and Wrist	148
52.	Averting Tennis Injuries: Midsection	149
53.	Miscellaneous Pearls	152
54.	Speed and Stamina	157
55.	A Winning Formula	161

Final Words — 162

Thank You — 163
Acknowledgements — 164
About the Author — 165
References — 166
Image Credits — 168

A principle is worth a thousand techniques

Warning – Disclaimer

The Lure of the Big Game is designed to provide insight on the game of tennis. It is not intended to provide all the information that is otherwise available to players through coaches, but instead to augment other forms of instruction. You are urged to seek a wide array of opinions, as no truly great player is the product of a single source.

Every effort has been made to include aspects of the game not inherently obvious or readily available. Tennis is a difficult sport, and competitive tennis is, at times, painful. Oftentimes, the reward is not in the game, but rather in the winning. For this reason, it cannot be recommended that having aspirations in competitive tennis is for everyone.

The Lure of the Big Game is to educate and entertain. The author and Today Publishing shall have neither liability nor responsibility to any person or entity with respect to any loss or damage caused, or alleged to have been caused, directly or indirectly, by the information contained in this book. No person or product mentioned in this book shall be held accountable as well.

Foreword

Wouldn't life be easier if everyone had an older sibling who faced life's uncertainties, met them, and gave you the answers, letting you avoid blunders and years of confusion? Rest assured, *The Lure of the Big Game* will provide you with competitive tennis wisdom and knowledge needed to win. Currently, there are many books that describe the game in terms of traditional techniques and psychology. However, after playing tournament tennis for over 12 years, I realize that conventional tennis advice is often inapplicable or difficult to understand.

This book will provide you with the tips and insights I discovered in my quest to improve so that you will not have to struggle as I once had. Instead of describing the mere appearance and attributes of a good tennis player, I will place an emphasis on the principles behind the methods, the ways to make them work for you and the direction to develop that winning game. You cannot jump from novice to advanced simply by imitating people. What a superb player does and how he or she does it are two very different things. The road to success is not as difficult as it appears, but without the right guidance, it can be very frustrating and circuitous.

I must admit that growing up, I scoffed at the notion of actually reading tennis books. They were simply too general and too basic. Always looking for insights to incorporate into my game, I asked better and more experienced players for the most important tips they picked up over the years and used in their game. However, many of them were reluctant to share their hard earned knowledge that gave them an advantage. In addition, most players rely on an overall feel of the game and are not aware of what they are doing.

Aspiring juniors and competitive neophytes fall victim to this learning predicament. They are left to struggle with the same tribulations and have to rediscover solutions and tricks for themselves. *The Lure of the Big Game* will change this. No cookie cutter advice. No empty truisms. Although you have never seen me on television, I am familiar with competitive tennis as it is played in juniors, in college and in clubs across the country. This is the game played in the trenches. I am giving you the insider advice that takes years to figure out.

Introduction

Once upon a time, there was a man who decided to climb a mountain. Starting off at the foot of the mountain, he began climbing. Progress was slow at first. Inch by inch, he would gain footholds and find new handholds along his way. Always keeping his eyes on the rock face in front of him, it was a grueling process. After many years, he climbed very high.

One clear day, when the sun shone especially bright and the clouds were thinner than usual, he looked up and saw the peak of the mountain for the first time. To his surprise, it did not seem that far away. Feeling proud of himself, he looked back at the ground and saw the great distance he had covered already. There were other climbers as well, but they were very far below. He felt very confident. Thoughts of greatness began to appear in his mind. How wonderful the view would be at the peak. What exhilaration.

These thoughts also troubled him. He grew tired of inching up the mountain, endlessly looking for footholds and handholds so diligently. The thought that the peak seemed so near turned into impatience. Finally, he could take it no more. The next day, instead of climbing slowly, always feeling for the next nook and cranny, he decided to begin jumping from ledge to ledge. This way, he figured, he would make much faster progress and the climb would be much easier. Although he would have to give up the handholds he had relied on, surely they had served their purpose already and would now provide the springboard for him to jump.

Looking up at the peak, he jumped as high as he could. In the air, he found himself a little higher than he was before. Being closer to the peak felt wonderful. However, at the top of the jump, he started falling back down and landed on a ledge below his previous foothold. Slightly discouraged but invigorated by the ease of the jump and the new height he experienced for a moment, he decided he had to try it again. So he did. Once again, he jumped high and was closer to the peak. And once again, he landed slightly lower than before. One big jump, he thought, that is all I need. Perhaps a few big jumps and I will be at the peak in an instant. Far better it is to jump for the peak than to never get there inching along.

This is how he continued for many months. Every day, he jumped and tried to land on ledges. Once in a while, he would succeed and this encouraged him. Most days, however, he kept landing lower and lower. Soon, he found himself pretty far down the mountain. Other climbers began passing him. He still could see the peak, but it did not seem as attainable as it once had. He kept jumping and landing lower. A year passed, and perhaps a few more months and another year. He found himself near the bottom of the mountain.

Negative thoughts haunted his dreams. Perhaps he should just slide all the way down the mountain and forget the whole thing. Sometimes he considered climbing inch by inch again. But this was very daunting for he remembered how tiring it was before. Not only that, he would again have to find his old handholds and footholds. On some days, he tried this. He tried to remember where they were. To his dismay, he had forgotten. One day, he lost hope. Nearly at the foot of the mountain, he had reached rock bottom.

All the other climbers scoffed at him now. He was so low. Some of them even doubted he had once climbed to where he said he had. There are better climbers nowadays, they said. You'll never catch up to them. Just move on. The man sat down for a long while and gathered his thoughts. No, he said. I will not step off this mountain knowing I never reached my peak. I will not be a climber remembered for how I came down the mountain. I will come down this mountain on my terms. And so he began again.

When the sun rose the next morning he vowed never to jump again. He felt with his hands; he felt with his feet. He searched not for old nooks and crannies, but for new ones. Each inch up the mountain was new. Each hold was new. He felt good again. He loved the feeling of scaling the mountain, feeling the solid rock beneath his feet. This time, he did not look up at the peak. He kept his eyes on the rocks in front of him. He ascended faster and faster. On some days, he passed other climbers. Some of them were not as nimble as he. Some were the naysayers and nonbelievers. And some of them were jumpers. All of them he passed. Inch by inch. And one day, when he reached for the next handhold, he felt nothing. He was there.

1

Finding the Will to Win

So you want to win tennis matches. Assuming you have a decent foundation, solid groundstrokes, consistent serve and volleys, the next step is developing the proper mind frame. I am sure you've read numerous articles about visualization or meditation. Chances are, if you're anything like me, these exotic theories sound great, but don't work half as well. I want you to let go of this pop psychology and listen to a more down to earth explanation of mental tennis.

> *Chess is war over the board. It's just you and your opponent and you're trying to prove something. The object is to crush the opponent's mind.*
> **—Bobby Fischer**

The first thing you have to understand and accept about a tennis match is that it is two hours of competition, pure and simple, in the most unadulterated, naked form you'll ever encounter short of a real fight. If you view tennis as merely a game of skill, you will never harness all of your inner fire needed to win the matches that matter. Two men enter a court, each to fend for himself. There are no coaches, no teammates, and oftentimes no spectators. There is no time limit. In the end, the only record of the match will be who won and who lost. There are no stories to tell, no condolences. Until you can swallow this, you are not putting yourself on the line to win.

What exactly is will power? It is a most fundamental question. Many people imagine will power to be determination and training. If my goal is to build a house out of matchsticks and I spend ten years doing it, sure, I have will power. However, will power in tennis is a whole different matter. There are two halves. Some people have one half, and some have the other. Very few have both. The first is the will power to prepare to win. To outwork the competition in training requires dedication and sacrifice. This weeds out most would be players. The second half of will power is more tricky. When all the six-month a year players have left and gone home, what separates the rest is the ability to out will another person face to face. When it comes time, two men for one prize, each will ask himself, how bad do I want it? Now, it is not a matter of training, skill or strength. It comes down to putting your ego on the line and a willingness to seize the prize. Many people do everything right, but at the moment of truth, they expect someone to give it to them. Understand this, you have to go out and get it for yourself.

Let me explain it to you in another way. As a young kid, I was never able to swallow pills. People would offer all kinds of advice: drink it with a big gulp of water, eat it with bread, imagine there was no pill. However, nothing worked. Every time I would gag on the pill at the last second. One day, I had an epiphany. All this time, I thought I wanted to swallow the pill, but in fact I really just wanted the pill to be swallowed. The difference was that I wasn't willing to make it happen, I just wanted it to happen by itself. No amount of bread and water would help until I convinced myself that I wanted to swallow the pill. You cannot hope it will come to you. It won't.

> Charley: *The only thing you got in this world is what you can sell. And the funny thing is that you're a salesman, and you don't know that.*
> Willy: *I've always tried to think otherwise, I guess. I always felt that if a man was impressive, and well liked, that nothing...*
>
> —**Arthur Miller,**
> **Death of a Salesman**

2

It's Time!

There is a spectrum of intensity levels you can have for a match. At the highest end, you have the level of the Hungriest Lion. Next is the Ultimate Warrior, followed by the Executioner. On the other end, often leading to defeat, is a series of Ambivalence, Frustration, Protection and Desperation. These last four can be grouped into one, Upset in the Making.

> *It's all fun and games until you're down a set and a break to P.S.*
>
> **—Adrian Bohane**

When analyzing each of these levels of intensity, I assume that your opponent is neither much more nor much less skillful than you. In these cases, your mind frame will largely determine the outcome of the match. Upset in the Making starts off with Ambivalence. You begin the match without urgency. Going through the motions, you hope your opponent will just go away. To an outsider, your attitude may not be evident, but you definitely know you're not ready for a battle. As your opponent sticks around and begins to win points, you get frustrated. Foreseeing doom, you start playing to protect your lead. Hoping your opponent will choke and give you the match, you play conservatively. Perhaps you woke up that day a little lethargic, not willing to go out and take the match. By this time, you feel the match slipping out of your hands. In an effort to regain control, you begin playing wildly, going for low percentage plays. More often than not, you proceed to lose the match ignominiously.

Ambivalence, obviously, is not the way to start off a match against a player about equal or slightly worse than you. A better mind frame is one of the focused Executioner. Finding this intensity will allow you to close out your opponent in a business-like fashion. At all times in a "routiney" match, you must have a sense of urgency. Your foot must always be on the gas pedal and you must never go into cruise mode. This is when Ambivalence sneaks in and steals defeat from the jaws of victory. If your opponent is on the verge, finish him off. The longer he hangs around, the more chances there are for something to go wrong. When playing with the Executioner mindset, focus on breaking the match into smaller tasks as described in the next chapter.

> *You owe it to your opponent to beat him as bad as possible.*
> **—Ty Tucker**

The level of intensity slightly higher than the Executioner is the Ultimate Warrior. Whereas the focused Executioner is best suited for players equal to or slightly worse than you, the Ultimate Warrior intensity is applied to players of an equal or slightly better caliber than you. Together, these two mind frames are sufficient to handle 95% of your matches.

> *Fear is your best friend or your worst enemy. It's like fire. If you can control it, it can cook for you; it can heat your house. If you can't control it, it will burn everything around you and destroy you. If you can control the fear, it makes you alert, like a deer coming across the lawn.*
>
> *I'm scared every time I go into the ring, but it's how you handle it. What you have to do is plant your feet, bite down on your mouthpiece and say, "Let's Go!"*
> **–Mike Tyson**

When you know that your opponent will give significant resistance to being closed out execution style, you have to shift up a gear. The first thing to do is give up some ground on your outlook of just offensively executing him. Assume an attitude of *hunkering down for a drawn out battle to the end.* Know that you will have to stand toe to toe and trade punches. Unlike the Executioner that relies primarily on focus, the Ultimate Warrior will have to call upon getting psyched up.

> *I no longer ask for the Big Game. I am thankful for the game I have because I want to win more than my opponent and it gives me the chance to do something about it – that is something special indeed. I don't ask for the tools to win, only the tools to fight, and I can handle the rest.*

Most people get pumped up and find the Ultimate Warrior mind before the match starts. *It is often hard to repeatedly summon enough adrenaline to get completely psyched up match after match.* The trick to this lies in classical conditioning. The psychologist Pavlov trained his dogs to reflexively salivate whenever they heard a bell because they subconsciously associated it with food. You must do something similar.

> *Uncas arose from the blow, as the wounded panther turns on his foe, and struck the murderer of Cora to his feet, by an effort, in which the last of his failing strength was expended.*
> **—James Fenimore Cooper, Last of the Mohicans**

Choose a set of songs that trigger a rush of adrenaline. Only listen to these songs before a match. After many matches, their galvanizing effect will become automatic. You will feel, almost nostalgically, that you can always summon the prematch mind frame. Your intensity is like a switch; *there are no gradients, it is either on or off.* Now, the real secret of being able to get pumped up time after time is not to do it in first person, but rather in third person. As you hear your music, imagine how other people see you. Envision them talking amongst themselves what a battler you are as they watch you play. Feel like you are making history and starring in your own movie. Look into the mirror and step outside of yourself for a moment. Have a hat or piece of clothing that invokes the transformation into a specific persona. See yourself as the Ultimate Warrior. Let your theme music be your cue. Relish the battle. You cannot let your spectators down. Find glory in the audience. Show off your fighting spirit. Even if you aren't sure if you have what it takes to be the Ultimate Warrior, if you pump your fists, grunt as if you're physically hurting your opponent, and play the role long enough, you will begin to believe it. Your music will start the ball rolling on a self-fulfilling prophecy. Turn the match into a war of attrition. And last but not least, don't forget, like in the <u>Last of the Mohicans</u> and <u>Braveheart</u>, the Ultimate Warrior suffers great pain and dies on the court. Play like it. Enjoy the role. Relish the atmosphere.

> *They fought—like brave men, long and well,*
> *They piled that ground with [enemy] slain,*
> *They conquered—but Bozzaris fell,*
> *Bleeding at every vein,*
> *His few surviving comrades saw*
> *His smile when rang their proud hurrah,*
> *And the red field was won;*
> *Then saw in death his eyelids close*
> *Calmly, as to a night's repose,*
> *Like flowers at set of sun.*
>
> **—Fitz-Greene Halleck, <u>Marco Bozzaris</u>**
> (qtd. in Cooper 339)

The final and highest level of intensity is the Hungriest Lion. Every once in a while, you hear about a remarkable feat in the news like a tiny woman lifting a bus to save her trapped baby. The power of adrenaline surging through your body is what drives the Hungriest Lion. Unlike the Ultimate Warrior, there is no trick to summoning this intensity. In order to find the Hungriest Lion, you have to convince yourself that your life depends on your winning this match. You want to win so much that you are literally shaking from mental exertion. Treat this match like your Wimbledon.

> *The Hungriest Lion – You sit in the car, the bathroom, the bushes or wherever you find silence. And you convince yourself that you want it so bad that it is 100%. You eliminate every bit of fear, anger, doubt, arrogance, excuse; you forget everyone you love, everyone you hate. You fill your veins with desire. And you don't leave that bathroom until there's no place you'd rather be and there's*

nothing in your life more important than winning. Then are you ready. And until the last ball flies out on match point, nothing else matters.

From the very beginning, pump it up and play not only to win, but to *steamroll your opponent. It is an all-out sprint.* There is both desperation and a thirst for blood in your heart. The problem with the Hungriest Lion is that it cannot be manufactured. It is difficult to summon this frenzied energy because each time you do, you have to reach higher and higher heights or else it will be lackluster and turn quickly into Ambivalence. Unlike the Ultimate Warrior, you are always living the moment in first person. Use the Hungriest Lion sprint sparingly. It is only for huge occasions. If you are not sure you have total life and death intensity, scale it down a notch to Ultimate Warrior or Executioner to avoid falling into Ambivalence.

Before a match, many people adopt the attitude of "I've trained hard, now I'll just let the chips fall where they may." Do not do this – do not accept defeat beforehand in order to relieve the pressure. There is no reason to lower your expectations – Run through the finish line.

Do not underestimate the effect your intensity has on your opponent. You may be able to overwhelm your opponent with shock and awe. The first couple rounds are always the best time to take out high seeds before they can acclimate to the tournament. Don't forget, there are few players who are mentally ready before a match to face the onslaught of a truly psyched up opponent.

Sometimes when I walk down the street I bet people will say there goes Roy Hobbs, the best there ever was in the game.
—**Bernard Malamud, The Natural**

There is something to be said about opportunities. Do not actively look for them because you often cannot recognize one until it is in front of your face. Take care of your business and simply capitalize on the opportunities that come your way. In a match or tournament, do not worry about how you are going to win. If you capitalize on enough of your opportunities, they will build up into something bigger. A good example is playing a really high-ranked player. Beating him may seem like a tall order at the beginning of the match. However, if you can stay with him, staying on serve, even if you are only hanging on by your fingertips, you may get an opportunity late in the set. At 15-30, 3-4 on his serve, if you recognize this slight window, you may be able to parlay it into a huge win. Don't underestimate small opportunities and don't expect them to happen more than once. Always be ready to jump on a chance to win something tangible, something that can never be taken away. You will always be able to say that you won it – it'll be forever.

3

Man of Infinite Focus

During high school and college, you will take many tests covering a huge amount of material. Instead of trying to tackle the entire textbook and voluminous pages of notes, break everything down and make a simplified study sheet of only what you need to memorize. By testing yourself with this, you won't have to confront such a daunting and indeterminate task. The important point is to clearly identify the task ahead of you or else you won't know where to start.

> *It's like taking a five hour final examination.*
> **—Bobby Fischer on a game of chess**

    A match is no different. It is a long event. It is often difficult to focus on winning and getting off the court as quickly as possible when you are just beginning. Nevertheless, focusing for a long time does not need to be so taxing on the mind. In fact, you can make it routine. The first thing to understand is that a tennis match is basically nothing except holding serve and breaking serve. Do not think of winning in the scope of a match. Simply reduce it into smaller tasks of holding and breaking serve.

    When you play, just try to win games. Assign holding serve once as one task. Then move onto the next task of breaking serve. Before you know it, you will find yourself at 5-4 serving for the set. Now, instead of thinking about closing out a set, think only about holding serve as a *self-encapsulated game*. You have held serve hundreds of times before. Just execute your task. This will eliminate the nerve factor.

    During the course of a match, you can even reduce the games into points. *View each point in the scope of trying to hold or break that game.* Focus on each point as how it relates to gaining a break point, a point to hold, or a first point lead. "Get this point to set up a chance at getting break point." "I need this first point to establish a lead in my service game." These are both good examples of focused thinking. Always aim for the next score: if you are returning 30-30, think "30-30, just gotta get it to 30-40...just gotta get a break point, c'mon!" A match will seem very short indeed and you will begin to see how individual points lead to games in no time.

    A classic example of this mind frame is the tiebreaker. All too often, players who gain an early lead 2-0 or 4-1 proceed to lose the tiebreaker. A lead of 4-1 or 5-2 may seem safe, but usually is only one mini-break of serve. Most people just try to play for a lead in a tiebreaker. They feel good if they are ahead instead of thinking of a lead in terms of holds and breaks. A false sense of security is the usual culprit in losing leads in tiebreakers. Holding serve and breaking serve each as self-encapsulated tasks is like going down a checklist systematically executing your plan and your opponent.

4

Understanding What You're Up Against

Tennis is unparalleled in its ability to expose the true psychological makeup and competitive nature of people. In the face of mano a mano battle, the everyday façade that hides their inner self dissolves away. After playing many matches, you will begin to recognize the several main categories that your opponents invariably fall into. Famous war tactician, Sun Tzu, once said, "Understand thy enemy." Tennis is no different. Understanding their psyche type will help you defeat them using your mind. Although a specific person may exhibit the characteristics of several different types, you will be able to see through their actions and attitudes. Keep these descriptions in mind when you sense your opponent's mental makeup.

TNT: As a child, this person most likely grew up in a sibling rivalry-type relationship. He and his siblings would compete for anything and everything including prizes, bets and parental attention. In life, he has a tendency to engage in arguments and try to win any head to head clash. The driving force behind this person is a truly competitive nature. After victory, he finds jubilation in proving his superiority. Invariably, he would have no obvious insecurities that would potentially make him vulnerable to other people's scrutiny.

      On the tennis court, this person feeds off of his innate competitive fire. He looks for any motivational spark to trigger a fierce competitive reflex. You must not awaken this sleeping dog. Very often, if you adopt a seemingly blasé exterior and avoid confrontation, you can slide by these opponents without much resistance. Act like you are going through the motions. Since their primary goal is to show others their superiority over you, you will not give them fuel to fight if your personality not challenge them. Be sure to maintain your composure after missing an easy ball or if your opponent wins a long point. Simply take the last point into account and focus on your goal of holding or breaking. Never bend over in exhaustion with your hands on your knees[1]. As soon as you display any weakness, the TNT player will sense blood in the water and use it to gain momentum. Act like it was just another point in executing your task. By the time he realizes you've slid by, it will be too late.

---

[1]Bracing your hands on your knees *does* help you take deeper breaths because it fixes your pectoral girdle and allows more chest expansion.

The Big Name: This is an unusual person. If it were up to him, the result of a tennis match would be predetermined by an accepted hierarchy. The so-called superior player would assume victory and the so-called inferior player would accept defeat. In this system, the exercise of the match is merely a formality. What drives this person is an innate repugnance of competition. For him, tennis represents conflict held at an arm's length away. Before matches, he pretty much decides whether he will win or lose based on the ranking and reputation of his opponent. Against presumed lesser players, he is resentful and indignant if they do not buy into his hierarchical scheme and actually expect to win. The Big Name is routinely a high seed at tournaments. He is usually very accustomed to people simply bowing down and losing to his reputation.

When you play against The Big Name, you have an excellent opportunity for an upset. You must look for any chance to instigate competition and show that you are challenging his status. Do not act like you are giving his game the respect he feels it deserves. Walk with authority and pump yourself up audibly. Psychologically invade his side of the court. His first reaction will be to put you in your place. However, if you can weather this storm, your chances of victory increase tremendously. Very often, he will proceed to tank the match if you can chink his armor. He will rescue the hierarchical conception in his mind by acting like you are not worth his effort. Even though he loses the match, he provides himself a way out. As soon as you sense the dam breaking, you must not lower your intensity, but rather pick it up another notch to ensure victory.

The Opportunist: If a ship were sinking, this person would be the first to jump off and would never stick around to fix the leak. He finds it very difficult to go out on a limb and always hedges his bets. In some ways, you could say he is complacent and small-minded. At the heart of this person lies an insecurity. In most cases, he talks trash and is especially boastful to cover up his vulnerability. This is what you must always keep in mind when you play Opportunists. Because he does not enjoy putting himself on the line, he will only compete hard if he feels he can defeat you. Subconsciously, he always considers whether the payoff of winning at the cost of losing is worth the effort.

> *Sometimes I feel like I'm on a ship that sprung a tiny leak in the middle of the ocean. Instead of just fixing it, everyone starts fighting for the lifejackets.*
> **—Frank Ng**

He sometimes uses trashtalking as a way of raising the stakes and payoff for winning. By your attitude, you must show him that competing against you is a losing proposition. Always maintain a strong, confident image. After winning the first set, play especially hard at the beginning of the second to let him know he has a long way to come back. Convince him that you are intent on getting a win and that he just happens to be in the way. Do not engage in trashtalking or even show him that you notice it. Keep your nose to the grindstone. If he feels that you are very determined and focused, he will lose hope and bail out of the match. You will encounter many Opportunists both in life and in tennis. As sociologist Christopher Lasch writes on the increasingly prevalent trend in America, "Self-preservation has replaced self-improvement as the goal of earthly existence."

The Good Camper: The Good Camper is more of an attitude than a personality type. It is a trap that anyone can fall into and one that must be avoided at all cost. In his heart, The Good Camper falls prey to defeatism. Going into a match, he plans his mind frame to prepare himself for a loss. Mentally, he thinks, "I'll just focus on playing good tennis," which leads inexorably to, "Well, it just wasn't good enough today" and "I just wasn't able to execute." The Good Camper always leaves himself a way out, a pressure valve. He shudders at the thought of doing whatever it takes to win and often finds succor in going 3 sets with good players. In his heart, he is committed to the game, but not possessed. There is a desire to win, but no inner need, no urgency.

Good tennis doesn't beat people. People beat people

Very often, the Good Camper will fall into another trap, the Martyr Trap. He works hard for the sake of working hard. Instead of concentrating on the end prize, he settles for consolation in the praise of others and self-congratulation for his unerring diligence. Do not plan your own private pity party. Being a martyr may make you feel good or even heroic, but it is not helpful and will not accomplish anything. Hard work does not guarantee anything and what you deserve is irrelevant. Instead, you must work because that is what it takes to achieve the end. Remember, there is no omnipotent arbitrator who doles out rewards for trying. Effort has no meaning in of itself and goes unseen until the moment you achieve your goal. The victory is not in having worked harder; the victory is in the trophy.

Brer Fox: Looking for trouble
Brer Bear: Just lookin'
—Disneyland, Splash Mountain

If you encounter a Good Camper across the net, defeating him is very simple. Play into his self-fulfilling prophecy. Psyche yourself up vocally and show him that you intend to win. To overcome his mental detachment, let him know that you are taking the match personally. Do not be afraid if he sets up beautiful points and seems carefree. When things go south, he will become frustrated, often admonishing himself and shaking his head. However, he always seems to lack a genuine anger. In the end, he will donate big points with easy misses and choke every time. Remember, do not just play; play to win.

There are tough players and nice guys, and I'm a tough player.
—Bobby Fischer

Do not fall for the Martyr Trap yourself. Once working hard ingrains itself in our minds, it becomes somewhat of an enigma. If you ever watch a dog chasing his tail, it is confusing whether the head is leading the tail or vice versa. It is easy to forget what you're working for. This is especially true in times of setback and disappointment. The tendency is to get frustrated and vent your anger by throwing away everything you still have. However, these actions and thoughts only make the situation worse. Although feeling sorry for yourself may feel good, understand that eventually you will have to pick up everything you dropped in your fit of depression. You know that you cannot spend the rest of your life moping, so don't dig a hole deeper than you need. When you decide that it is time to wipe away the blood and tears, don't start with the attitude of fixing something. This will only engender rueful thinking. Your approach should be to accept the present situation and try to make it better. You cannot always count on fixing something, but you can always make something better than it is now.

> *Deserve has got nothing to do with it.*
> **—Clint Eastwood, Unforgiven**

Society provides many instances of the problematic Good Camper syndrome. By losing sight of your end goals, the process itself becomes the perceived objective. The overwhelming result is a failure to achieve what was originally intended and much confusion on the actual and apparent reasons of breakdown. In the classic example of child rearing, Hilde Bruch writes, "The common error of psychological advice is teaching parents techniques of conveying to the child a sense of being loved instead of relying on their innate true feelings of love."

> *The guy who wins the race is always someone who is able to admit to himself that he cares and actually wants to win the race.*
> **—Ty Tucker**

Clearly, you can see that glamorizing and finding assuagement in the processes themselves will only produce poor outcomes. This is especially true in tennis competition and training.

The Prisoner's Dilemma Cheater: The famous economist, John Nash, formulated a game theory called the Prisoner's Dilemma. In short, the story goes like this. Two robbers are captured by the police. However, there is not enough evidence to incriminate either robber on a full count. With no corroboration, each robber will serve only one year. Trying to pit them against each other, the police question them separately. To each, the police offers a lesser sentence if he testifies against his partner in crime. If one robber remains silent, but gets ratted out by his partner, he will get 5 years as the sucker. If they both squeal, they get 3 years each. Now, each robber must carefully consider his options. Obviously, cooperation will result in the best outcome for both. However, the question remains: can you trust another person?

As a tennis player, you will see various aspects of this game play out with wins and losses as currency. There is no bigger headache than to play the Prisoner's Dilemma Cheater. At no time should you trust this person's actions during a match. Be ready for mind games galore. Always trying to get the best of the situation at your expense, he will adopt several approaches. He may feign seemingly sincere respect at the beginning of the match to engender similar respect from you. Late in the match, he will use your deference to psyche you out of a win. He may pretend to tank in an effort to evoke similar lackluster from you. He may try to intimidate you. In any case, you must always refrain from cooperation or risk being the sucker in the end. He is often a skillful hook. You should deal with him like poison ivy. Do not even attempt to joust with him at any level. Set your sights on your goal while being wary for his shenanigans.

<u>The Showboat</u>: This person plays tennis for the spectators. Usually the most prolific bragger, he finds joy in high rankings, dramatic shots and big wins. Showboats are often what people call "shotmakers," although not all shotmakers are showboats. Oftentimes, the designation of shotmaker is attributable to the selective recollection of the one miraculous shot made instead of the three unglamorous unforced errors. Instead of noticing the dynamics between him and his opponent, the Showboat is more concerned with what image he is sending to the onlookers. Oftentimes, he is despised for his arrogance. Surprisingly, this arrogance is a potent psychological weapon. Some of his opponents so hate him, they are consumed with this emotion that they cannot focus on winning the match. With each spectacular overhead the Showboat hits, they become further enraged and lose control. Another bunch of his opponents are too feeble to challenge his arrogance. They simply defer from confrontation with a half-hearted effort and hope not to bear any of his disrespect.

He has humor, but no wit.

—**Dave Schilling**

   To defeat the Showboat, you must conquer both of these demons within yourself. The most important point is understanding that the Showboat thrives on momentum. You must try to destroy his waves. Motivate yourself quietly lest he try harder, thinking you're trying to show him up. Do not simply be a punching dummy for him. Many people advocate stalling as a good tactic. However, a better way to counteract his momentum is to create your own. Just as his highs are very high, so too are his lows. Very often, he will exhibit negative body language to show the crowd that he is playing well below his capability in order to save his reputation. At this point, he is breaking down. Know that at crucial, pressure filled points, you will always have an opening to turn the tide. The Showboat, no matter how impressively he is playing, will get tight when his desire to win wedges itself before his need to look good.
   Tennis is filled with Showboats. Take heart in knowing that by beating them and remaining humble yourself, you can serve as a sort of "Universal Humbler" by capping their arrogance in your presence.

No sir, I body clowns.

—**Ben Kirksey**

5

The True Champion

> *White Fang ceased only when he had tired himself out. He could do nothing and he could not understand. Never, in all his fighting, had this happened. The dogs he had fought with did not fight that way. With them it was snap and slash and get away, snap and slash and get away... The bulldog's method was to hold what he had, and when opportunity favored to work in for more. Opportunity favored when White Fang remained quiet. When White Fang struggled, Cherokee was content merely to hold on.*
> —**Jack London, White Fang**

Every once in a great while, you run into an opponent without any mental deficiency. Live this match as if it's your last and you will understand everything you'll ever need to know about mental toughness.

Dog fighting is illegal in America, so I hope this is all new to you. There is no breed of dog more legendary in the pit than the American Pit Bull Terrier. The will of these dogs remains one of the most admired characteristics in American folklore. For years, people have sought to breed the ultimate fighting dog by isolating and combining the attributes most important for victory in the pit. The insights of these breeders into the Pit Bull's mind are very useful in understanding the human competitive psyche. It turns out that many dogs exhibit remarkably similar traits to people.

All dogs have some level of Prey Drive, the instinctive reaction to chase a moving object. There is no thought process nor motivation needed to trigger the dog's response. It is simply a reflex arising from deep within its evolution. We all know what it is like to play fetch with a dog. The game usually lasts a long time until the dog succumbs to exhaustion and physically cannot continue.

In humans, this instinctual behavior is found most prominently in the TNT personality. The TNT person is driven to compete as an automatic response to being in a highly competitive environment. Essentially, he is a machine programmed to perform at his highest capability until he breaks down. At first glance, the TNT person appears to be the optimal form of competitor like some sort of Terminator. However, he has a flaw. His willingness and level of desire to compete is not a measure of his ability to win. He does not treat competition with enough gravity. To him, competition is merely an activity like knitting, talking on the phone or bagging groceries. It is a response, the mindless carrying out of a routine, nothing more, nothing less. Winning a tennis match requires personality, intellect, emotion, and a recognition that in a mano a mano confrontation, your survival is on the line.

Envision this scenario, a pack of wild dogs is feeding on a carcass. Two of them begin fighting over one piece of meat. The first stage of this conflict begins with intimidation and threat displays such as growling, raising their hackles and baring their teeth. These actions are recognized as aggressive behavior. If neither dog backs down, they resort to fighting. However, this physical encounter is always very brief with one of them backing down before any serious injuries are inflicted.

What can we glean from this thought experiment? Dogs will instinctively avoid a hostile confrontation. While some dogs use aggressive measures, others will tuck their tails and lower their heads to ensure their well being. In the wild, they know that any injury could be debilitating or fatal. An actual fight is almost always an unnecessary risk to take. From this, we see that Aggression, and similarly, Submission, are survivalist traits. Instead of indicating a willingness or ability to fight, they are actually the opposite. They arise from fear. It is a savage game of Chicken. Evolution has chosen those individuals that can best threaten confrontation and then avoid risk at the last moment. The pressure of natural selection has long dwindled those individuals that actually sustain injury and fight regardless of outcome.

> One day, if you ever meet a man without any scars, it means he never fought for anything he believed in.
> —**Chuck Norris, Walker, Texas Ranger**

These instincts to avoid conflict and its risk are present in humans. Since confrontations in which the chance of physical injury is very rare, people have taken it to a new level. Instead of fearing for their body and survival, people often fear for their ego and are afraid of putting it on the line. Other than TNT, all of the above-described personalities can fall into either the Aggression or Submission crutch. They are merely psychological ploys players set up for themselves to protect their ego's survival. It is impossible to completely eradicate these two tendencies from your personality, but reducing their influence on your frame of mind is crucial to winning. In dogfighting, an aggressive or submissive dog was known pejoratively as a cur.

> Without discipline, no matter how good you are, you are nothing. One day, and I might not be around, you're going to meet a tough guy who takes your best shot. He'll keep coming because he's tough. Don't get discouraged. That's when discipline comes in.
> –**Mike Tyson**

The dog most sought after by breeders is the so-called "cold dog." When threatened and even attacked by another dog, the cold dog resists fighting and shows neither Aggression nor Submission. In essence, it is unafraid and feels unthreatened by his opponent. This is known as Gameness. A deeply game dog is slow to fight, but once started, will never stop fighting until death. It has the desire to succeed and overcome despite any hardship or against any odds. Gameness is the will to win. In the pit, the game dog refrains from engaging until it is absolutely necessary. This quality enables it to defeat more aggressive opponents. A dog that starts the fight strong and tries to finish it as early as possible will wear itself out. It is not easy for one bulldog to severely injure another. As the hard chomping dog loses steam, its aggression will quickly turn to submission. This determination and willingness to put survival on the line is what defines true Gameness.

In humans, this is a largely invisible trait. Society and its many facades often hides true grit and courage behind the hype and image. While posers must rely on intimidation and other theatrics, the deeply game individual has the confidence that he is not afraid of laying it on the line. This, oftentimes, is his only advantage. For him, tennis boils down to his worth. He vows never to let an opponent best him. He fully understands the implications of confrontation. He does not have an easy way out of the match and is thus a reluctant competitor. He fights out of a certain necessity, a necessity to win. It will end, either in complete victory, or complete defeat. After a win, there is no jubilation, no celebration, only relief. He has fought to live another day. Perhaps this quality is mere folly, destined to be edged out by evolution, or maybe nature left a precious few individuals to carry on true Gameness. Have Gameness. Be a combat dog.

Let us examine the actual dynamics of a dogfight. Before the match, each dog is washed by the opposite trainer to ensure no chemicals were applied to hamper the opponent. The dogs are then washed with the same water and dried with the same towel. The pit is a square measuring 14 feet along each wall. A scratch line is drawn two feet from opposing corners. The dogs are held in each corner facing each other. Many dogs, the more aggressive and submissive ones, will growl and whine at each other. The game dogs, on the other hand, will quietly await the command.

Once the referee signals their release, the dogs rush at each other and begin fighting. It is not common for one dog to run out of the pit before even beginning the match. The referee oversees the fighting and when one dog gains an advantage, causing its opponent to turn its head and shoulders away, he calls a turn. The dogs are separated and brought back to their respective corners. The referee says, "face your dogs," and the down dog is released. It has ten seconds to get up and reach its opponent's scratch line, indicating a will to fight. As soon as the released dog crosses the scratch line, the opposing handler can let go of his dog at any time. The fight continues indefinitely until one dog refuses to scratch. Clearly, the fight is a contest of gameness. A dog that always attempts to scratch in any condition is considered the most prized fighter.

Just as life is full of veils and veneers, tennis strips them all away until only your true character remains. Since it is very difficult for one dog to kill another, the winner is decided by scratches and numerous face-offs. Similarly, a tennis match is comprised of many, many points. There are no quick wins. You must show resolve and indicate your will to win over and over again. But most of all, what makes tennis harsher than any other sport is its indefinite duration leading always to a winner and a loser. To understand this, you must follow my logic carefully here.

We often see young children and juvenile animals exhibit Gameness, the unwillingness to quit, in their playful interactions. However, play by design is not harmful: it never determines a winner or loser for humans and never results in serious physical injury for animals. Because there is nothing at risk in play, it is not as difficult to have Gameness. As people and animals grow older, their play turns into actual competition. Whether it is for a trophy or a piece of meat, the confrontation always ends with a winner and loser. Here, it is infinitely harder to have Gameness when there is something at stake. Tennis simulates individual adult confrontation while every timed sport, though head to head, merely represents play. Both teams keep playing until time runs out. The game clock essentially provides a built-in mechanism for an easy way out. The winner is not forced to completely dominate the loser, and the loser is not forced to fully relinquish and submit. In tennis, as in dogfighting, there is no clock. You yourself determine your own fate. You must answer the scratch every time and struggle it out with your opponent until the bitter end. There is no compromise, nothing is spared. If you cannot win, then you must accept loss.

Tennis is a Zero-Sum Contest. What one person gains is exactly proportional to what the other loses. You cannot win until you are prepared to take something directly away from your opponent.

6

Trashtalking

In competition, there are always two forces at work in a player's mind: the hatred for losing and the love of winning. Although there is always a measure of each, consider a polarized scenario in which one player is driven completely by the hatred of losing and the other by the love of winning. Who do you think has the stronger motivation to win? Surprisingly, it is the player with the hatred for losing. He competes to avert the imminent detrimental effect on his well-being while the other player merely competes to gain an optional reward. In other words, if the first player does not win, he is worse off than when he started; if the second player does not win, he simply lost the opportunity for the additional boon of winning.

A couple years ago, I used to practice with a lower ranked player and subsequently, it was always expected that I beat him. Unfortunately, he was a habitual trashtalker. This was one of my biggest pet peeves. Trashtalking cost him nothing because he was supposed to lose anyways. However, it increased his ego payoff if he actually won. For me, his trashtalking raised the stakes higher and higher because if I lost, it would be even more damaging to my ego. Practice became very stressful.

Did he do the right thing? While his trashtalking "got into my head," it also made me more determined not to lose. However, it increased his payoff if he did manage to win albeit with lower odds.

The player who is nervous and cautious about jumping headlong into competition is not cowardly, but rather has a good sense of the gravity associated with the situation. He knows that if he enters the contest, he must win. The prize of winning must be greater than his hatred for losing. On the other hand, the player who exudes bravado and talks trash either is ignorant to the implications of losing or already expects to lose. Essentially, he has nothing to wager, yet still gambles.

There is one exception to this rule. If you up the ante on yourself by talking trash, making a loss even more devastating, you provide yourself additional motivation to win. On days when you do not feel like competing or when the stakes are not very high, you can turn the smallest contest into a major conflagration. Consider Michael Jordan. As one of the greatest competitors ever and most prolific trash talkers ever to step onto a basketball court, Jordan used his hatred for losing as an indefatigable source of determination. From his experience of being cut from his high school basketball team, Jordan vowed never to come up short again. It is no coincidence that the toughest competitors are often those who have been slighted at one point in their life and now refuse to let anyone get the better of them. Use these quiet embers and you may discover a surprising strength within you.

As a point of common sense, when you are winning a match and sensing that your opponent's will to fight is dissipating, do not act in any way (gloating, cheating, etc.) that would give him an incentive to fight. If he wants to tank or slink away, take the win and let him go.

One sign that someone is new to competition is if he or she gloats while winning. Everyone who is used to competing on a regular basis knows that there comes a time, perhaps the very next instance, that they are on the losing side. No one wants to have their opponents gloat or rub it in their face. Remember, the telltale sign of competition inexperience is not getting bent out of shape or being a sore loser, but rather gloating while winning.

7

The Crosscourt Figure-8 Play

I don't believe in psychology. I believe in good moves
—**Bobby Fischer**

U nderstanding and applying this play will reward you with countless points from the baseline. (For the sake of explanation, assume you are right-handed playing a right-handed opponent.) If your groundstrokes are inferior than your opponent's, this play will maximize the effect of your shots and make him play up to his highest potential to beat you. If you are the superior groundstroker, this play will eliminate luck from the equation and make it nearly impossible for an inferior groundstroker to win points consistently. Most matches are lost by either giving away too many free points or falling repeatedly into a disadvantageous pattern. This crosscourt play allows both of the factors to work in your favor.

It began to feel as though I was playing against chess itself.
—**Walter Shipman (on playing against Fischer)**

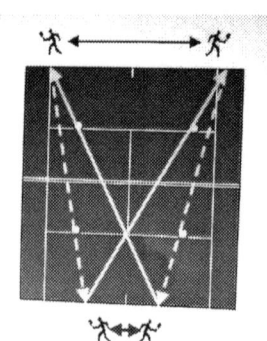

Think of the play like a python. The snake uses its coils to hold its victim securely, patiently increasing the pressure as the hapless animal struggles to extricate itself. The figure-8 crosscourt pattern is invaluable to your success as a baseliner. Ideally, you should seek to hit crosscourt shots while your opponent hits down the line, resulting in the ball traveling in a figure-8 path. Because your shots are crosscourt, they are always traveling away from your opponent, carrying him off the court. Conversely, his down the line shots will naturally be heading back towards the center of the court and you. *This will make him run a much further distance than you to cover shots.* In addition, the crosscourt shot is a much safer shot because the balls will travel over the lowest part of the net and there is a longer court to hit into. If you hit a forehand while standing on the ad side of your court, you should take this ball crosscourt to their forehand and forgo the inside-out shot (at least for now). The same is true for your backhand on the deuce side. *Always be cognizant of the figure-8 geometry and you will develop an intuitive sense of point dynamics.*

The basic idea is to continually pound balls into the crosscourt corner. I use the word pound because instead of simply rallying, you are trying to use the strength of your shots to force your opponent into the next part of the play. After a while, your opponent responds with a shot he tries to return crosscourt, but because of the strength of your shot or the weakness of his stroke, he leaves the ball somewhere in the middle or down the line. Immediately, you should look to pound this ball crosscourt with your opposite stroke to start him moving in a figure-8.

At this point, he can do two things. If he returns your shot down the line, pound it crosscourt to the other side. After several times on the wrong end of the figure-8, you will have him right where you want him. If he manages to scramble and return your shot crosscourt, simply engage the crosscourt play again on that side. Do not worry if you feel that you have lost an offensive opportunity. Many people try to force a winner because they don't want to lose the offensive advantage. This is the wrong idea. You have not lost an advantage because your opponent is increasingly tired. Let your advantage accrue and do not give up superior positioning. Simply reset the figure-8. Very often, he will go for a reckless shot, the low percentage play you want him to try, especially when he is fatigued.

There are several misconceptions people have about the crosscourt figure-8 play. Do not fear that your opponent knows where you are hitting every shot. You do not need to surprise your opponent. Very often, you will surprise him due to the simple fact that you are hitting it to the same place every time and that he keeps guessing you are going to change it up. Once you establish the pattern in his mind, you can truly fool him later in the match. Do not feel you have to hit it to the open court simply because it is there. This is a common mistake. Number one, most players anticipate well and are conditioned to cover the open court. They will be ready for it. Number two, it opens up angles on your side of the court. Number three, it is usually a lower percentage shot. Do not hit it to the open court unless you are sure it will do damage and you know you will not miss it.

The biggest sticking point of the figure-8 play is getting away from the "hit it into open court" or "make your opponent run" tunnel vision. Let's say you hit a forcing shot to the sideline. Your opponent is slightly stretched out and returns it crosscourt. Most inexperienced players would hit the next ball down the line to the "open" court trying to press their advantage as soon as they taste blood. However, your opponent is conditioned to cover this ball, and easily gets to it since your shot is curving to the middle of the court. Instead, you should hit that ball back crosscourt and make your opponent stretch out enough so that he can only return it down the line. *Now*, hit it into the open court (crosscourt) and put him in a figure-8. Your shot will be curving away from him, putting you at a distinct advantage. Or, if you wanted to be tricky, you could hit his down the line ball back down the line. This will really wrongfoot him because after you establish the figure-8, players will be conditioned to sense the figure-8 pattern impending whenever they leave a ball short and down the line.

When applying the crosscourt play, you do not have to recover all the way back to the middle. While he may have an idea where you are going to hit the ball, you are forcing his hand as well. By not hitting the ball randomly about the court, you are limiting the places he can hit it and reducing the chances of him wrong footing you. You always have to recover just enough to the middle to be sure that you can cover the down the line and hit a forcing shot crosscourt where he won't be able to hit another forcing shot. In essence, you are trying to either force a weak reply off your crosscourt ball, or you are baiting him to try a low percentage shot down the line. Do not worry if he hits a winner once in a while. It is just luck, and in the long run, he will miss a lot more than he will make.

One very common application of the crosscourt figure-8 play is against baseliners who like to run around their backhand with big forehands. Oftentimes, people try to beat these players by trying in vain to get it to their backhand. The forehand bashers simply hit harder and harder inside-out forehands and move farther and farther into the backhand corner. Eventually, they set up a ball they like and turn on it for a winner to the other side. The best way to counter the big forehand is by actually hitting to their forehand corner with a crosscourt forehand of your own. *Instead of trying to play it up the line to get it to their backhand, where the ball will always curve back to their forehand, you should play it crosscourt where it will move away from them.* He will not be able to hurt you as badly with the forehand from the true forehand side of the court. His balls will always be heading towards you rather than tailing away as with the inside-out forehand. Now, you have opened up his backhand corner. When he goes for a forehand down the line, you can attack his backhand with your crosscourt backhand. Not only will he then have to hit a backhand, but he will also have to come up with it on the run. Also, make sure you get your backhands to his backhand and not let him hit forehands from the middle of the court.

The biggest scourge of winning competitive tennis is unforced errors. Simply by reducing your mistakes, you can increase your success twofold. However, do not misinterpret true consistency as merely keeping the ball in play. *The truly effective form of consistency is being able to set up your play while not giving away free points in the process.* It does you no good if you put your opponent in a disadvantageous position, but lose three out of four previous points trying to get there. There is another misconception about being consistent. True consistency is not about making 20, 30 or even 50 balls in a row. It is about making one more ball than your opponent whether it is after 4 shots or 100 shots.

Always have a feel for the figure-8 pattern and you will intuitively know when you are safe, when you have an opening, and when your opponent has made a mistake.

If your opponent has a weak side, there are many different ways to take advantage of it, but some are more successful than others. You could rally to it until he misses; you could try to hit through it; you could approach the net and make him pass with it. However, if it is a long-standing weakness and your opponent is either an experienced or highly ranked player, he has probably adapted fairly sophisticated strategies to cover it up. The best approach to such a situation is to use the figure-8 as you normally would. Be cognizant that his weak side will allow you to put him in more figure-8's because he will not be able to get his weak stroke crosscourt as well. He will leave a lot of them short or down the line – exactly what you want.

Conservative and careful yet consistent tactics have been used to win battles for many years. Consider the phalanx formation used by the Greek army in the Dark Ages. It was a tight column formation, usually ten men across the front rank and ten men deep. Each side of the phalanx was protected by soldiers holding their shields edge to edge and pointing their spears outwards much like a cross between a turtle and a porcupine. Used as an offensive infantry formation for hand-to-hand shock combat, the phalanx would advance at a deliberate pace on the enemy, smothering them with an impenetrable wall. In early BC, the Greeks used the phalanx to defeat a larger Persian army that used the traditional, yet disorganized, charge and massacre tactics. In other wars, even when the Greeks had superior numbers, they resisted simply rushing into battle and relied on the phalanx to offset any chance of an upset defeat. Like the Greek phalanx, apply the figure-8 play and you will maximize the highest potential of your groundstrokes no matter what your skill level.

Don't move until you see it. Don't move until you see it.
Here, let me help you [clears the board of all the pieces so they are staring at the board itself]
—Ben Kingsley, Searching for Bobby Fischer

The figure-8 crosscourt play is not merely a strategy based on a series of shots (like a series of moves of chess pieces). It is intrinsic to tennis itself (like the chessboard itself).

8

Troubleshooting the Crosscourt Figure-8 Play

If the crosscourt play does not seem to be working for you, there are several ways to troubleshoot it. If it seems that your opponent is hitting forcing shots down the line and you are just reacting to them, you are not pounding your crosscourt balls hard enough. Ideally, he should not be able to play high percentage offense down the line off your balls. What you want to avoid is him being able to meet your balls at their peak and hit downward into your court. You can prevent this with depth, topspin or by pounding your shots downward so that he has to hit up to you.

    Another scenario that could cause trouble is if your opponent starts hurting you with extreme angles off your crosscourt shot. These angles will make you scramble way off the court so that you cannot cover down the line on the next ball. In this case, you definitely don't want him to dictate the same play to you. The two strategies you want to avoid are trying to hit an extreme angle of your own and going for a winner down the line. The former is bad because it allows your opponent to shove the ball down the line and come to net. The latter is bad because it is low percentage, the ball will be tailing back to him, and all your opponent has to do is bloop the ball to the open court since you're way out of position. The reason you can't shove the ball and come to net off of his initial angle is that he won't be as far out of position as you are when you hit the extreme angle off of his extreme angle.

    So what do you do? You can try to pound the ball deep crosscourt, but this is often a difficult shot and if you leave it a little short, you are deadmeat. A good player will bunt it down the line with decent consistency even if you do get it deep crosscourt. The best thing you can do is to hit a hard ball right down the middle of his court, preferably jamming him. It does not matter which stroke he takes it with. He will have no angles to work with, and it will be low percentage for him to go for a winner off a hard struck ball. The shot to the middle of the court is also a fairly high percentage shot because you don't risk hitting it wide and it is off a slow shot by him. From here, you can reset your crosscourt play. Do not be afraid that your opponent will keep using sharp angles to extricate himself from your play. The crosscourt angle off a hard pounded groundstroke is as low percentage as going for a winner down the line. Let him try it.

Another scenario that could cause trouble is if you feel that a player is using the same crosscourt play on you and that you will break down and relinquish a midcourt ball before he does. To ease the building pressure crosscourt, you can hit a safe rally ball down the line and continue the crosscourt pattern on the other side. The main thing with this response is that you have to hit the ball down the line on your terms. If you feel his shots getting heavier and heavier and soon you will leave a ball short, you have to switch up the sides before you are forced to. This will make him restart and rebuild the crosscourt pressure. Hopefully he will become impatient and go for a lower percentage shot.

As soon as you hit the rally ball down the line, you have to get ready for a crosscourt reply to the other side and not let this shot by your opponent be so forcing that you leave the next ball in the middle. You should be able to recover to the other side quickly because you know you are switching up the sides before you even hit the down the line ball. At this point, your opponent will usually hit it crosscourt, but if he is tricky, he will try to wrong foot you and hit one back up the line. This is a tough shot to cover, but it is low percentage on his part, and if he leaves it somewhat in the middle, you can get him into a figure 8.

One way your opponent can try to foil your play is by slicing his backhand crosscourt. *Do not get into a slicing contest with him* and slice it back to his backhand. Most likely, this is what he is looking for and will take your slice and chip it and come in. You should take his first slice and slice it down the line to his forehand. If possible, slice it with a little inside-out spin so that it tails to your left, away from his forehand. Although most people's forehands are their strong side, they will not be able to generate offense. If they hit your slice up the line, take your backhand and pound it crosscourt to establish a figure-8. (If your opponent's slice pulls you way off the court, hit your slice back crosscourt to avoid falling into a figure-8. The described play applies best when your opponent's slice lands in the middle of your ad court and not near the sideline.)

A player may resort to slicing their backhand to catch his breath. Make him pay as soon as he tries it. Covering a backhand slice down the line with his forehand will be very taxing on his legs. It will be difficult for him to get around the outside of the ball and return it all the way crosscourt. When he leaves it on your backhand side, pound it crosscourt to get him in a figure-8. By taking your slice up the line a few times early in the match, it will open up the opportunity to take slices crosscourt later since he will be leaning to cover his forehand. He definitely will not be able to chip your slice and come in because his momentum will be on his heels.

Basically, the only way to truly foil the crosscourt figure-8 play is to prevent someone from even starting it. Chip and chargers take high risks coming to net. However, they force their opponents as well to raise the risk on their shots and to hit passing shots. Unlike the occasional net rusher, the chip and charger does not become discouraged if he is passed several times early in the match. Even if he wins only 55% of the times he comes in, the more he does it, the more significant that 5% becomes. By continually charging the net, he forces his own percentage play onto the baseliner.

9

Variations on the Figure-8 Crosscourt Play: Holding the Inside-Out Forehand

When the only tool you have is a hammer, everything starts to look like a nail.
—**Adapted from Abraham Maslow**

On a hot day, holding your shots can be devastating to your opponent's stamina. The principle behind holding a shot is to disguise where you are going to hit the ball. Your opponent cannot lean to one side and simply has to react. It is especially taxing on his legs because he has to quickly push off from a stationary inertia. If you are rallying crosscourt with your backhand, your opponent may leave a floating ball in the middle of the court. Instead of using your backhand to pound it crosscourt, look to hit a forehand. Run around way to the left of the ball as if you are setting up to hit an inside-out forehand. *You should exaggerate the footwork in order to sell the inside-out forehand to your opponent.* At this point, he will be expecting a penetrating shot towards his backhand corner. However, you can turn over your forehand at the last second and pound it into his forehand corner instead (see diagram).

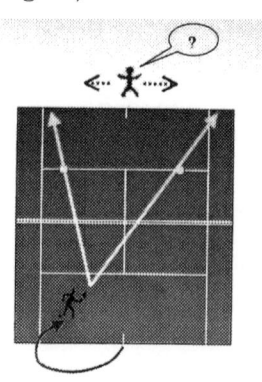

This play enhances the crosscourt figure-8 pattern. Although you are basically still doing the same play, you keep him honest by giving him the inside-out forehand to worry about. An important tip to remember is that holding the forehand works only if you have a ball appropriate for hitting inside-out. You cannot run all the way around a ball if it is traveling from your left to your right, only if it is floating from their backhand to your backhand.

10

Variations on the Crosscourt Figure-8 Play: Sneaking the Forehand Down the Line

After rallying crosscourt for several balls, many players will not recover all the way back to the middle. You can take advantage of this by setting up the forehand approach down the line against slower and less mobile players. When in a forehand crosscourt rally, look for a reply from your opponent that is crosscourt, yet slightly slower and shorter. Step into the court and with an abbreviated groundstroke, block the forehand flat and down the line. By taking it early, you will surprise your opponent and keep him on the move. Follow the path of your shot and approach the net (see diagram). Do not simply run to the middle of the net. This is a common mistake. If you hit your forehand well, he will not be able to beat you with a sharp crosscourt passing shot. Cover the down the line pass and look for a defensive floater or lob from your opponent.

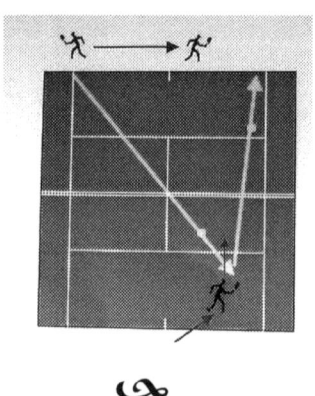

11

A Note About Hitting Balls At Their Peak

There is one attribute that all aggressive baseliners have in common. They always make contact with the ball when it is bouncing at its peak. Obviously, if someone hits a lob, they cannot hit it when it is 25 feet in the air, but for most normal groundstrokes, they meet the ball at its highest point. The peak of the path of the ball is unique. If you notice, there is always a split second when the ball seems to just hang stationary in the air; it is neither on the way up, nor on the way down. It is difficult to perceive this special moment when watching from the side, but from a player's point of view, the peak is very evident.

    Hitting the ball at the peak has three advantages. Number one, it takes away your opponent's reaction time and makes it more difficult for him to read where you are going to hit the ball. Number two, it immediately punishes your opponents for leaving balls short. Finally, you are able to hit down on the ball into his court, making him hit a more defensive shot up over the net. Even if you do not hit the ball hard, your opponent will feel pressure and sense that you are attacking him. Catching the ball at the peak is how you can use your footspeed to attack. When you let the ball drop and hit it after its peak, the path of your groundstroke will be more parabolic and more defensive in nature. This will reduce the effectiveness of your shot even if you are striking it hard.

    If you ever watch Agassi play, it seems that his opponents are always hitting the ball to him while he dictates the point and runs them around. This is because Agassi always hits the ball at its peak. In fact, he hits it on the rise, an even more effective method that is very risky and not suitable for anyone not named Agassi. Remember, hitting balls at their peak will give you offense and allow you to take away your opponent's time. Conversely, you can give yourself more time in defensive situations by letting the ball drop and hitting a more parabolic shot.

    Many players have trouble realizing when they should be on offense or defense. A simple rule is based on the ball's peak. If your opponent can hit down into your court, you should adopt a defensive posture even if he is slightly out of position or behind the baseline. On the other hand, look to create offense on your next shot if your opponent catches the ball below the net and has to hit up to you.

12

Using the Crosscourt Figure-8 Play for Defense

Just as you can apply the crosscourt play for offense, so too can you use it when your opponent is attacking. The number one rule for playing defense is *avoid letting your opponents hit run-around (aka inside-out) forehands*, or inside-out backhands for that matter. The problem with the run-around shot is that they make playing defense very difficult. You have to respect his ability to hit the run-around forehand to either corner. Unlike the ordinary down the line forehand, the inside-out forehand will run off the court as you chase it over a longer distance. *At all cost, if you can hit the ball past the service line, you should make sure you get the ball to your opponent's groundstroke that is designed for that half of the court.*

> *Chess is a matter of delicate judgment, knowing when to punch and when to duck.*
> **—Bobby Fischer**

Usually, players cannot hit an outright winner off their first inside-out forehand. They use it to set up a weak reply and then knock off a forehand crosscourt for the winner. When you recognize your opponent is in an offensive position and you have to play defense, do not panic. Simply drop back farther than normal behind the baseline to give yourself some time to react and room to run. Some people advise against this because you have more ground to cover, but this is only true if you don't understand the angles of the court. You will not have a chance to run if you stand right on the baseline and cannot react to the ball. Do not get beat before the ball even bounces. It will slow down once it hits the court.

> *Don't panic in the guard.*
> **—Royce Gracie, Brazilian Jiu-Jitsu Legend**

As a rule, always lean and cover towards the side of the court where your opponent's shot would be tailing away from you. If he has a short backhand, cover your backhand side and give him the lower percentage down the line. Notice in the below diagram, you should stand to the left of the hashmark to cover the crosscourt ball. By backing up, you will have time to track down the down the line shot because it will be heading back towards the court. You also are taking away his easy crosscourt putaway where his shot will be running away from you (his only placement for a winner is marked by the dotted line). The same idea is applied if your opponent has a short forehand.

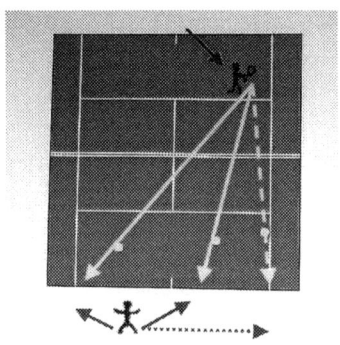

If your opponent has a run-around forehand, cover more to your backhand side because if he hits it to that side, the ball will be jumping away from you. Very few people can hit their forehand from their backhand corner to your forehand corner with sufficient topspin and angle to make the ball jump away from you. Indeed, it is difficult to use topspin to generate offense unless your opponent is already slightly out of position. Once you get to his inside-out forehand shot, try to hit the ball crosscourt and make him hit a backhand with it. This will let you return to the crosscourt pattern and neutralize his offense. *Many people play defense incorrectly by hitting balls up the line.* Unless it is very deep, you are not improving your situation. *He will simply put you in the wrong end of a figure-8 and you will still be stuck in a defensive posture.* Only play defense up the line if you cannot keep the ball in the court any other way. Always know beforehand where you are going to hit the ball. Remember, the crosscourt pattern is your friend. If in trouble, try to return to this pattern and make him hit low percentage winners down the line.

When you are playing defense, return your opponent's attacking balls crosscourt instead of down the line. This will prevent you from falling into a figure-8 and decrease the amount of ground you have to cover chasing balls. In addition, by not having to potentially cover / chase balls that are curving away from you, you will not have to "lean" towards covering the open court as much – protecting yourself from being wrongfooted. Understand that when you play defense crosscourt, if your opponent chooses to play offense down the line on the next ball, all you have to do is get to that ball and play defense crosscourt to the other side. This reduces his offensive advantage because although he is attacking, he is on the wrong side of the figure-8. If your opponent attacks the ball down the line and follows it to net, all you have to do is get to his shot and roll it crosscourt to his feet. He will then have to play a low volley down the line (which puts him on the wrong side of a figure-8 at net) or he will play a low volley crosscourt right back to where you already are. With an opponent coming to net off of a down the line approach of your crosscourt defense, it is essentially a footrace. You are racing to get to his approach and roll it crosscourt before he can get to net and cut it off. However, you are at a distinct advantage because if he wants to win the footrace, he will have to anticipate / guess the roll crosscourt and get a head start, which allows you to play a down the line pass behind him. Or better yet, you can play a forehand topspin lob down the line catching him not only moving towards the net, but to the wrong side of the court as well. Notice that the forehand topspin lob is set up perfectly (when your opponent approaches to this side) because you can easily curl it using your body momentum moving to the right as you move to cover the approach.

General Rule:

If your opponent has an attackable ball – fall back behind the baseline to give yourself time to run and track down his shot. Be ready to cover his high percentage targets.
  1. *If he attacks and stays back, look to play deep crosscourt defense and return to the figure-8*
  2. *If he approaches the net, look to hit a short, low crosscourt ball to his feet to make him play a low volley*
     a. *Recover back to baseline and look to pass or lob off of his volley.*

13

Neutralizing a Big Weapon

Consider this example, let's say you have a good forehand and you are struggling against an opponent with a seemingly devastating backhand. To effectively neutralize this situation, you have to first understand how your opponent is winning his points. It probably seems that he is hitting backhand winners at will. However, this can be misleading. Most likely, he uses a strong crosscourt backhand to your weaker backhand to draw a short response and then slams a putaway with his backhand. The trick to handling this is to protect your backhand corner from the get-go and make sure he cannot draw the weak response with his crosscourt backhand. Do not worry about his down the line backhand. If he takes his strength to the open court, it will be to your strength and you will be able to counter with an attack of your own. When he does choose to go there, make sure you take your strength crosscourt to his weaker forehand. *The idea is to prevent him from hitting his strength twice in a row.* If you can achieve this, few opponents will be able to mount effective offense against you.

When analyzing previous points, do not fall into the trap of simply noticing the last shot in the rally. Too many players base their entire strategy on the stroke their opponents miss or hit a winner with, paying no regard to the pattern leading up to it. Oftentimes, that final shot is a strength or weakness not in itself, but rather in the scope of the situation as a whole.

In the same vein, do not conclude that you should formulate a strategical pattern in the warm-up or during the match based on your perception of your opponent's weakness. At high level tennis, reliable weaknesses are not so much strokes themselves, but rather patterns and situations your opponents are susceptible to. With this in mind, always start matches using patterns that, in your experience, are fairly universally effective and only adjust them if you can definitively pinpoint your opponent's weakness.

14

Two Defensive Shots to Consider

If your opponent has you stretched out to your backhand, a helpful shot to have is the backhand slice. Primarily, you should use the slice off a ball where you are way off the court and have to play defense. A sliced backhand travels through the air more slowly and will give you time to recover. The most important aspect of hitting a slice is keeping it low over the net, which makes your opponent hit up on the next shot. Whether he sneaks in to volley your slice or stays back and tries to generate offense, he will not be able to slam the next ball downwards into your court.

Another use for the slice is to foil a particularly hard-hitting opponent. It is difficult for him to hit pace off of a slice because he must add extra topspin to get it over the net. Because it is very difficult to effectively slice a hard struck ball, you must hit your slice before he has a chance to start pounding balls. Remember that the slice must serve a purpose such as setting up your forehand. It is only an intermediary tool and cannot win points by itself.

Another neutralizing shot is a topspin roll high to your opponent's backhand. Like the slice, this shot is best used with slower balls that are positionally tough to handle, that is, when you are way off the court. Because it is high and has topspin, your opponent will not be able to hit it at its peak, giving you time to recover. In addition, if his backhand is his weaker shot, he will relinquish any thoughts of generating offense.

The most important aspect about the high topspin roll is that you must use it on your terms. Do not wait until you are in desperate straits to try this shot. You want to use it while you still have other options, so your opponent will not be able to anticipate it. Do not let him force your hand into hitting it. As soon as you feel your opponent building up a positional advantage and pulling you slightly off the court, use it to stymie him before he can back you into a corner.

If you struggle to play defense, one option you may want to consider is placing lead tape on your racquet. The extra weight will help you achieve depth on your shots even if you can barely reach the ball. It will improve your return of serve immensely as well because it allows you to block the ball back and still get good pace. Try putting a strip of lead tape at nine and three o'clock on your racquet head (assuming the handle is positioned at six o'clock). There will be a noticeable difference in the weight of the racquet head. Feel free to keep adding tape until your first reaction when picking up the racquet is not the heaviness of the head, but rather the lightness of the grip. Not only can lead tape help you hit heavier strokes, but it can also help you to control your opponent's shots. Remember, you don't need to hit the ball harder than your opponent, you simply need to be able to handle his pace.

15

Effective Passing Shots

There are several important aspects to hitting passing shots. Number one, you want to pass your opponent early enough and often enough to dissuade him from approaching later in the set when each point is more valuable and there is more pressure on you. Number two, passing shots are difficult, especially if your opponent is fully at net. The easiest time to hurt the volleyer is when he is in the transitional phase from the baseline to net. Once he is at net, he has a positional advantage and it is significantly harder to pass even from a neutral ball. *Your goal should be to make him hit a defensive low volley from the service line or no-man's land.* He will have to volley up to you and you will be able to hit an offensive passing shot. You are in trouble if you find yourself hitting passing shots up over the net off of low balls.

Assuming he has made it to net, you have to keep your options in mind. *Do not always feel you have to keep the ball out of the netman's reach.* It may be difficult to wrap balls around his wingspan. Remember to keep good pace on your passing shots. Oftentimes, he will not be able to react quickly enough and will miss the volley. Another tool in your passing shot briefcase is topspin. If you can make your ball dip below the net, you will always get another look at a passing shot. A low dipping shot should be your default choice if you have no other options. Your opponent will have to play defense off a low volley and you can pass him off the next ball.

Even though the net rusher is forcing the action, you can remain in control of the point by keeping him guessing with your passing shots. Early in the match, you should establish an effective passing shot, the short crosscourt topspin roll. This is a relatively safe shot that leaves him with the few options. It is your best bet to discourage him from coming in any more. Once you feel that your opponent respects the topspin roll, begin to show him the lob. Because the lob is not very high percentage on an important point, use it in the middle of the set just to let him know you have it. It will keep him honest and not let him stand tightly to the net with impunity. If he begins to anticipate the lob and rock on his heels, it will open up more passing shots. In addition, jumping up to hit overheads is physically taxing and will take out your opponent's legs. Once he gets tired, he will not be able to put them away and will begin to miss. It is important to remember to not attempt an outright pass off of your opponent's approach shot. *Your goal should be to make him pop up a low, midcourt volley so that you can pass him off the next shot.* In addition, it is difficult to hit an angle or lob off of a hard struck approach shot.

In general, pace and disguise are your friends when trying to pass down the line. If you try to sneak the ball by your opponent, he will probably swat it away for a winner. Your best bet is to pound it down the line even if it is within his reach. It is a short distance, so he will have less time to react. Using the crosscourt roll early and often will set up the down-the-line pass later. *On a big point late in the match, you do not want to hit the crosscourt roll and let the ball pass in front of your opponent.* If you leave it a little too high and he cuts it off, it will be an easy winner. Hopefully you used the crosscourt roll frequently enough already and set yourself up to use the down-the-line pass in the clutch.

Many players are missing the lob from their passing shot arsenal because they have the wrong idea about it. You cannot think about a lob simply as a high parabolic shot that goes over the volleyer's head. You will miss many such misconceived lobs long and have many overheads slammed unceremoniously in your face. There is much more to it.

The most effective lob is hit with your forehand deep into what would be their backhand corner. Think of the lob passing high over their backhand volley. At no time should the ball be on your opponent's right side. This makes it very awkward for him to hit an overhead. Ideally, you should impart left to right sidespin onto the ball, helping it back into the court once it passes over him. To work on this shot, try running to your right as if hitting a running forehand and then hit the lob. The momentum of your body moving to the right should help with this curling action over his backhand side. The diagram shows what you should visualize in your mind even though the actual physics are slightly different.

Perhaps the best trick to hitting it is *not to think about the lob in terms of a ball traveling up, over someone and then back down. Think of it only in terms of a ball traveling to the right and then curling back into the court over their backhand side.* It is much like a "banana" kick in soccer.

Note: Flat offensive lobs are generally ineffectual and ill-advised. Flat lobs for defensive purposes usually only work if thrown up high enough to mess with your opponent's timing and if the sun is a factor.

16

Holding Serve with a Plan

Being able to hold serve consistently is largely based on *having a plan*. By not having to actively manufacture service games and by reducing each one into merely a matter of execution, you will help eliminate the chance of choking. In addition, by doing your job and holding serve, you will put pressure on your opponent's service games. Remember, most of the time when you are broken, your opponent does not play four brilliant points. He usually earns only one while bad luck and you donate the other three. You must be stingy and not give away any dumb points.

> *Best by test.*
> **—Bobby Fischer on 1. e4** (when asked why he always uses the same opening move)

This begins with the serve. I cannot stress the fact enough that you should not just hit serves randomly. If you have a pattern in your mind, that is, knowing where you are going to hit your serve in different score scenarios like 0-0, 15-0, 30-40, 40-30, then you will not second guess yourself on what serve to go for at that point. Oftentimes, players wrestle with the option of "playing it safe" or "having some guts and going for it" at crucial moments. *If you have a designated serve for a certain point, you will never have doubts and will be able to go for it with a peace of mind.* This is very helpful in the mindset of having a plan when you execute holding serve. Do not fear that opponents will pick up on your trend. The players that do take note usually only recognize the service patterns you use on big points. In any case, the serves you use on big points should be based more on high percentage rather than on surprise.

Generally, it is best to save your best serve for important points. This keeps it fresh and does not let your opponent see it too often. If the situation is not extra crucial, do not use your favorite serve. A good service pattern is to serve primarily to one spot to make your opponent lean that way, and then keep him honest by beating him occasionally to the other side. This way, you are always setting up the next serve, rather than scattershooting them.

Doug Bloom, an old coach of mine who was notorious for wearing out an opponent, gave me this piece of advice. *When you suspect your opponent is tired after a long point, an effective serve to use is the slice out wide.* It is a higher percentage shot than a bomb up the T and will not give him extra rest or the opportunity to gather himself while looking at a second serve. Usually, he will be slow to react and will simply reach for it. The slice also opens up the court for the next shot, giving him a lot of territory to cover when he is tired. There is only one caveat with this serve. Whereas most players with a Western forehand grip can only return the wide slice serve back up the line or in the middle of the court, players with Eastern forehands can hit it back wide crosscourt with relative ease. Many of these players leave that corner seemingly open to bait you to give them a stretched out forehand.

The slice out wide at 15-40 is a good choice because of two inherent dangers. Other than the fact that you are on the verge of being broken, your opponent feels the cushion of two break points and is free to go for a low-percentage winner. In a normal situation, this would work in your favor because the product of numerous low percentage risks and the likelihood of him stringing several together is very small ($\frac{1}{4} \times \frac{1}{4} \times \frac{1}{4} = 1/64$). However, a one time gamble is not as low percentage ($\frac{1}{4}$). The slice out wide is safe in this scenario because it stretches him out and allows you to control the rest of the point. The goal at 15-40 is to not give your opponent the chance to take a chance. The only way you can do that is by making sure he cannot fully set up on a waist high ball and take a good crack at it. Keep your slices low, your loops high, and your groundstrokes deep. Once you reach 30-40, your opponent feels the pressure of his one remaining break point and will most likely not risk a low percentage shot. You are safe to apply your normal high percentage gameplan in this situation.

One particular pattern that works well is hitting spin serves to the unorthodox side of the service box. Usually, a kick serve is hit to the right side of the box (the server's right) while slice serves are hit to the left side. If you can hit a "fake kick" to the left side of the box and a slice serve to the right that jams your opponent, they will take your opponent by surprise. He will not be able to take a full swing at the return, often shanking it if he tries to take the ball early.

A common problem players have on their service game is double faulting. One effective training tool for correcting this is to play a couple matches using your second serve as your first. Try to play without missing a single first serve, increasing the pace and spin on this serve as much as possible. Then, you will develop confidence in that particular serve. You can throw in a real first serve with the mindset that it is a "free serve" because you are playing off of your other spin serve anyways.

Another dilemma players face in a match is what to do if they are missing a lot of flat first serves. Do not give up on this serve by choosing to spin in a first serve just to get it in. The only reason to do this is if your opponent is attacking your second serve effectively. By abandoning your flat first, you will never get any free points for the rest of the match. Your opponent will always be ready for your spin serve and seldom miss it if he does not have to worry about a flat bomb. In addition, you will not be able to go back to your flat serve later in the match because you will have lost your confidence and rhythm with it.

There are several technical tips on the serve worth noting. On the slice serve, you should try to keep your nonserving arm up as long as possible until it is naturally pulled down right before you contact the ball. This helps in two ways. Number one, it keeps your body erect and allows you to hit a true slice. If you do not stay upright, your racquet face will inevitably come a little underneath the ball and impart some kick into your serve, which will detract from the sliding effect of the slice. Doug Bloom advised his players to envision the slice as if you are throwing a football spiral. You want the racquet face to slice fully to the right of the ball. Number two, your nonserving arm can help aim the slice. Imagine your nonserving arm like a pole in front of you. As you can see, your arm will bisect the service box into two halves from your point of view. When you serve, think about hitting the slice into the box left of your pole arm. Without it, it is difficult to hit a spot in the court with your slice. Most often, your slice will land errantly about the box.

There is an easy trick for hitting slice serves up the T on the ad side. Try tossing the ball across your hashmark, fairly far to the right so that it is on the deuce side of the court. Now, when you go to hit the slice serve up the T, you will be able to make it tail away from the returner because the ball will travel in a right to left direction (your deuce box to the T in his ad box) rather than a left to right direction (your ad box to his ad box). Likewise, you can use the same technique for kick serves up the T on the deuce side.

Developing a good kick serve is one of the most difficult aspects of tennis. Many coaches explain it in terms of clock faces and arm and body contortions. As long as you are aware that the kick serve is basically a topspin serve, there are three points you must remember to make the learning process as easy as possible. First, keep your nonserving arm up as long as possible. Second, swing upwards with all your strength. Keeping your nonserving arm up will keep the ball from going over the fence. Third, try to make the ball go to the target with kick as *fast* as possible. Most people will advise you to swing as hard as possible, much like a first serve. This, however, conjures up images of flatness. A better image is to focus on the *speed* of the *ball*. Make the ball go over the net and reach your target quickly with *fast spin*.

If you are having trouble learning the kick serve, you can start off with an intermediary type of spin serve. Try tossing the ball slightly behind your head and hitting it with spin. You do not have to attempt any specific type of spin (most beginners will naturally slice across it). This combination of a kick toss and slice swing will give you a decent and safe "spin" serve – which can be somewhat tricky if returners are only used to seeing pure slice or pure kick.

On a general note, coaches always say, "use your legs on the serve," but this is quite ambiguous advice. How does one actually apply this? A good way to think about this in terms of your body. Use the push off from your legs to lift your body into the air as if you're jumping. When you strike the ball, your body should still be headed upward from your jump. Conceptually, think of your body giving the ball lift so it will go over the net. Sometimes, it is helpful to imagine your body lifting the ball even higher than the point at which you made contact with it.

One simple addition that can immediately improve your first serve is adding lead tape to your racquet head at nine and three o'clock. Feel the weight of the head of the racquet generating power when it strikes the ball. *It is important to use your muscles in synchrony with the movement of the added weight.* Think of it like pushing a pendulum or a playground swing. Using force in the right rhythm can increase the momentum while applying force at the wrong moment can decrease the momentum.

Weight training can also help you develop pace on your serve. Lateral pull-downs behind the head are an effective way of working on the muscles needed to hit a powerful serve. However, be careful not to use too much weight and always maintain good form.

17

Returning Serve

While the serve is a huge part of the game, the return of serve is equally important in breaking. Being able to break is based in large part on reducing the number of free points your opponent gets off his service delivery. *You should never miss a second serve return.* Stand back and give yourself room behind the baseline on second serves. You will not get beat by tricky spin if you have time to judge it and let it finish moving around in the air before you hit it. Do not be afraid that giving up room will enable your opponent to angle you off with his second serve. He would have to aim for the lines, and this is a low percentage shot. A good second serve return strategy is to always show "close" (stand close to baseline), then back up as he is tossing the ball (unless you think he is going to serve and volley).

You should aim the second serve return deep and high over the net with plenty of topspin. This will completely neutralize the point. Do not attack second serves unless you are making at least 75% of your aggressive returns. Theoretically, if your opponent misses his first serve, you should consider your odds of winning the point at least as high as 50%. Even if you feel you are pressuring his second serve, you will never break serve missing any more than 25% of them outright. You must make the most of the points started on his second serve since he is supposed to win his first serve points anyways.

On the first serve return, you should stand closer to the baseline than on the second serve. This is because he can afford to aim for the lines and angle you off the court. The key to returning serve is having an idea where the serve is going and lean towards it before you have to react to the ball coming off his racquet. You can "feel" a certain serve coming with your body and sense it in a number of ways.

Think about where your opponent likes to serve. On noncrucial points, this can be a little hard, but after a few big points, you will have a good idea where he goes in the crunch. Do not let his variety of serves on noncrucial points distract you from detecting his tendencies on big points. Note that if he beats you with a certain serve several times, he will probably put that into his memory bank, and if he does not keep going to the well immediately, he will late in the match.

Another way to sense his serve is by watching his service motion. Use the warm-up to get a feel for it. After several games, your subconscious mind will begin to anticipate which serve is coming. Don't try to spot specific characteristics, but look at his entire body in general. Watch his toss. Look at what grip he's holding by the angle of the racquet before he tosses. Most of all, try to *sense the twist of his body*. Very often, this will reveal if a kick, slice or flat serve is coming. Only seeing a lot of service motions will help you develop this skill. But above all, once you mentally picture the direction of the spin, feel the serve and lean with your body, not your mind.

Sometimes servers are very discreet, and reading their serve is impossible. This is often the case with good serve and volleyers. Instead of getting into a guessing game with your opponent, which you'll invariably lose since there's more than two places he can serve and only one that you can pick, you need to simply react to the serve. Still, you are not completely at his mercy. Before he serves, pick a target where you are going to hit your return. Whether the serve comes to your backhand or forehand, keep the spot in mind throughout the serve and return. This can be deadly against serve and volleyers because they rely on being in control, having the whole point premeditated and forcing your whole hand. A good rule of thumb with this play is keeping the return on the same side of the court that you're returning, that is, if you're returning in the deuce court, aim to pass him to his backhand side whether it comes to your forehand or backhand.

If your opponent employs the kick serve and volley strategy, do not be intimidated. Stay close to the baseline (taking the return *slightly* earlier than normal will not give him time to close the net) and simply hit a soft return that lands short (do not float it high though). While this return would be an easy putaway for a baseliner, it will make the serve and volleyer hit a low volley. Remember not to take a full swing at the return or try to pass him outright; it is difficult because you do not know exactly how much kick to expect or if he applied a touch of slice as well.

Being confused with spin serves is really your own fault. What you need to do, especially on second serves and with lefties, is *in your mind's eye, consciously see which way a particular spin will bounce*. If you see a lefty kicking the serve, see the ball bouncing to your right before it even comes, so that it will never surprise you. Do not be fooled by a lefty hitting a kick to your left and thinking it'll bounce like most spin serves to that side usually do (left). It will jump as all lefty kicks do: to your right.

Very often, lefty servers like to set you up with their serve. They will keep slicing you to your backhand and then ace you flat the other way when you are ripe for the taking. Against this strategy, you need to lean towards the slice. Do not commit to it, but feel the slice coming, and if it is flat the other way, just react to it. It is better to feel one serve and react to another than to react to two serves. Your mind cannot move as fast if it has to be ready to cover two places. If it already shuts out one option (the slice), it can focus all its attention on the one remaining (the flat). Focus on keeping your eyes glued to the ball even while it is still in your opponent's hand. Remember, *the return of serve is more about feeling the serve coming with your body than reacting to it with your mind.*

   In summary, an effective flowchart for returning serve is as follows:

1) Read the your opponent's toss for spin and probable location.

2) If he disguises his toss or uses his toss placement to intentionally trick you, read the twist in his body. These first two tricks will take care of 90% of fairly advanced players.

3) For opponents who can completely disguise their serve, have a feeling of where he will serve based on the point situation. Most good servers have individual tendencies to use the same serve on specific scores in the game.

4) If all else fails, pick a spot for your return and cover the serve which your opponent makes with the highest percentage.

18

Opportunities in Holding and Breaking Serve

Holding and breaking serve often boils down to how you recognize and handle opportunities. Do not show your opponent everything on less than crucial points. In fact, if you can hide some of your capabilities, all the better. Sometimes winning takes nuance and guile. For instance, if he does not think you can handle the kick serve and volley to your backhand, let him win some of those points to bolster his confidence. Then, on a break point, burn him when he goes to the well. Treat serving like playing chess. Taking your queen out on the 2nd move of the game and trying to lay waste to your opponent without using your knights and bishops will only lead to her gradual ineffectiveness. Use your best serve judiciously.

But let us begin with how to handle break points against you. Getting an effective first serve in is very important. It allows you to start the point on your terms and apply your high percentage play. In order for your opponent to break you, you have to make him come up with a low percentage winner. However, do not simply play passively and wait for him to make an error. The idea is to slowly advance pressure on him like trapping a fish in an aquarium. Do not chase him around or make any sudden jerky moves. Simply corner him and force him into your net. Besides going for an ill-advised winner, the next worst thing you can do is let him force his own high percentage play onto you. Do not let him take control of the point. In addition, try not to leave any balls in the court where he could potentially go for a winner. Try to keep your slices low and your groundstrokes deep to eliminate the one shot kill for him. If he goes for it, the fate of the match is in his hands, and you have left yourself out of the picture.

Taking advantage of break points for you is the similar idea. Basically, you want to try to control the point with your high percentage play and break your opponent down. Against an inferior player upon whom you can impose your play, this is your best bet. You will be surprised how many players go for ill-advised shots in crucial situations because they cannot take the mounting pressure or do not have a plan. However, if you are facing a better player, you cannot completely let him apply his favorite strategy. Play along with his play, giving up a little control. You should always be looking for him to give you a ball you can go for the one strike winner. For me, it was the backhand down the line. I would let him get me into his play, but never giving up too much ground. The idea was to make sure the backhand down the line winner was still an option. Once he gave me a ball with which I could set up my backhand, I would spring from my semi-defensive posture into immediate offense. Sure, the backhand down the line screaming winner was usually less than a 50% proposition, but with the better players, I took the point into my own hands and took my chance with my favorite shot.

An excellent opportunity to establish a break is the very first game of the match. By letting your opponent serve first, you can surprise him with your stinginess. *Most players donate points at the start of their matches expecting mutual sloppiness from their opponent.* If you can make the break of serve stick the rest of the first set, your opponent will come to regret his early match folly and may never recover.

Never underestimate small opportunities. In close matches, if you let them slip away, you may never get another chance. Even if you have triple break point, play that point as if he will hit service winners on the next two points. Make every opportunity count. A missed opportunity could easily turn into an opportunity for your opponent. At the National Claycourts in 1996, I could not convert on five, albeit nonconsecutive, match points in a second set breaker against WL. As close as I was to closing him out, WL was equally close to evening the match. After squandering all my opportunities and energy, I got rolled in the third set. An important lesson is that it's not about how many opportunities you have, but rather on how many you capitalize on that makes the difference.

Even though they are commonly thrown around, catch-phrases such as "serve your way out of it" and "take a chance on his 2nd serve" almost never apply. Unless you're on the pro tour, this type of advice is usually low percentage. As a general rule, when the match gets close, become even more disciplined and decide to play each point strictly "by the books," that is, going with your most proven and practiced plan of action. Even if you feel heroic or lucky at the time, you will regret going for the risky shot more often than not. *Crunch time is the time for high percentage decisions.*

19

The Backhand Principle

For most tennis strokes, there are many different ways to hit them. However, the two-handed backhand is unique in having relatively few variants. Basically, a person will fall into one of two categories of players: those with good backhands and those with weak backhands. There are few players whose backhands are neither a liability nor a weapon. If you do not have a natural backhand that you've cultivated since childhood, there are several approaches to develop a backhand you can hit with impunity. The following descriptions are listed from most advanced to most basic.

Do not think of the backhand like hitting a shot of your own per se. *Focus on using your backhand to control your opponent's shot and not so much on hitting your own shot.* If you want to hit a hard backhand, think about "controlling it harder" not hitting it harder. If you want more topspin, think about "controlling it with more topspin" not "hitting more topspin." As you become more comfortable with this, you can reduce the spin until there is just enough to retain control.

The best way to achieve proper topspin on the backhand is to *envision your racquet traveling only in a direction perpendicular to the path of the ball* (straight up). As your opponent's shot travels horizontally and you make contact, the ball should hit your strings as they are traveling in an upward motion. The racquet movement should be broken down into a large vertical vector and a very small horizontal vector. Think about the top of the frame cutting through the air upwards rather than having the air flow through the string bed in a horizontal swing. A common misconception about the backhand is that your body acts as a sort of hinge on a swinging door. Think about how hard it is to control the direction of the ball when playing a pinball machine. You should not try to rotate and hit the ball like a flipper. Instead, think of your racquet like the spaceship in the old arcade game, "breakout"; you have master control on ball even though the ship only moves in a plane perpendicular to the path of the ball.

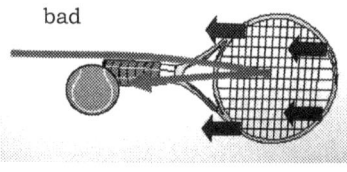
bad

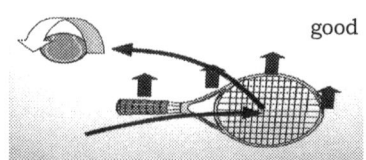
good

With a good forehand, it is easier to play effective offense. With a good backhand, it is easier to play effective defense (because a weak forehand is easier to defend than a weak backhand).

To hit a ball flatter, simply slow down the racquet moving upward so that the strings brush the back of the ball less. Do not increase the horizontal vector. To achieve this upward motion of the racquet, you must adjust your body. The lower the ball and the more spin you wish to impart, the more closed your stance must be. *Instead of 'turning your shoulders' per generic advice, simply turn and face the side fence with your entire upper and lower body.* There is no need to coil your torso. Your swing should naturally travel from your left hip to over your right shoulder with no resistance. You will naturally hit through the ball; there is no need to think 'through,' only 'up.' Remember again, conceptualize topspin as it is used to control your opponent's shot and not to give your own shot topspin. Adjust your body and stance rather than your swing to accommodate the height of the ball. The racquet should travel the same path relative to your body on every ball. Once you reach an advanced level, you will conceptualize your entire backhand stroke as simply controlling your opponent's shot and not creating a separate shot of your own.

Another good and more basic way of learning the backhand is to keep your body (both above and below the waist), both of your arms, and the racquet as one piece. Instead of each part moving separately as part of a jointed system during the backhand stroke, they should remain rigid relative to each other. Too many players erroneously envision the stroke as *one half of the body twisting or uncoiling against the other*. This is simply what it *looks* like, not what **really** is happening. In order to strike the ball, let *your entire body (as one piece) uncoil against the ground* to generate force and control. This will **engender** a good feel and solid fundamentals.

For a child, one of the best ways to develop a good backhand is to picture Monica Seles. In the early 90's when she dominated the Grand Slams, every time she hit a backhand, it appeared that she was catching the ball high over the net and pounding it down into her opponent's court. By visualizing your backhand more as pounding it down into the ground across the net rather than as a stroke with a horizontal projectile, you will naturally begin to utilize your entire body. Most players, especially those who do not learn as a child, never develop a backhand that capitalizes on their full body strength because they are always afraid of the ball traveling too far and sailing out. Focusing on slamming the ball down into the court eliminates the possibility of hitting long. Obviously, you cannot hit down into the court on low balls, but this is something to keep in mind for any ball above the net level.

The backhand, like every other shot in tennis, is about getting the right principles instead of micro-managing every technique. A truly good player can hit his backhand open stance, closed stance, jumping in the air or even sitting in a chair. He does not reach this mastery by having a specific technique for each scenario, but rather by applying the same principle every time.

20

The Forehand Principle

The forehand is the most technically liberal shot in the game. With all the countless variations that work, it would be difficult to identify a specific way to guarantee success for everyone. There is no one motion or technical detail that is at the heart of every lethal forehand. While good footwork and weight transfer are characteristic of all excellent forehands, they are not the cause. As in mastering any shot, you must remember to focus on the process of improvement rather than the final appearance. Use the environment and natural selection, that is, your opponents and your results, to guide your metamorphosis rather than a conception of the ideal forehand (see the chapter on The Evolutionary Way of Learning). While the wings of insects, birds and bats are very different, they all fit their surroundings perfectly. Flight was not their goal. It just happened through their common quest for survival.

Every tennis player already has a forehand of some sort. Suggesting a drastic change at this point would only set back your evolution. Work with what you have. Remember that diligence will yield stepwise improvement and that it is the only secret that reveals all the other secrets. The real gold lies not in any stroke, any accomplishment, any skill or any idea. It lies in you and your future potential. Many great movie producers are one hit wonders because they try to duplicate their success by imitating their first movie instead of harnessing their innate originality. They forget that the true gem lies not in the one strike of brilliance, but in the genius of person who created it. You do not have to imitate yourself to recreate success.

Practically all of baseline bashers with dominating forehands you see were at one point in their career pushers. Whether they simply kept balls in play forever or relied on counterpunching, they learned the value and efficacy of consistency. Truly, pushing is the precursor to the aggressive baselining. As the pusher rises higher in the ranks, he begins to compete and practice with better players who hit him off the court. Each day, this forces him to *raise the pace of his shots, but always holding onto his consistent base.* Eventually, he is able to crush the ball without ever missing. *If you want to be a baseline basher, don't fall for the common trap of hitting balls hard, spraying them across the curtain and expecting them to start falling in eventually.* After making obscene numbers of unforced errors, all you will learn is how to miss.

In practice, you should hit the ball as hard as you can while still expecting the ball to stay in, preferably to your target. When you miss, it should come as a surprise. If you feel as if you are rolling the dice every time you hit the ball, you are not doing anything for your game. This is the difference between pushing the envelope and simply going for broke.

One way that you can develop the feel of hitting winners with your forehand is by attacking second serves with your forehand. In this situation, it may help to practice with players weaker than you and who have slow second serves. This will give you confidence in punishing short balls with your forehand.

The principle behind success is gradual improvement through many little adjustments rather than one or two huge revelations. Work on consistency and let the competition raise your game. As your body gets more and more used to your form, it will continually and naturally optimize itself. Every time you manually or consciously change your stroke, your body must tear down what it has already solidified and rebuild itself, all for a shot in the dark at an unproven alteration.

The basic principle behind the forehand is very similar to that of the backhand. As the ball travels towards you in a horizontal fashion, your racquet face (in your mind's eye) should travel in a vertical fashion such that the string bed brushes up the back of the ball. You should think of the forehand, much like the backhand, as simply controlling the spin. The pace and forward movement of the ball will come naturally and inevitably as a result of your stroke – hitting through the ball (in a horizontal direction) per conventional advice happens by itself and is not necessarily something you need to think about. The most natural grips to facilitate this are: forehand – semiwestern / "frying pan"; backhand – continental (right hand) and left hand flat against grip (playing only a limited role in the stroke).

For adult beginners, it may be easiest to conceptualize the forehand stroke from the standpoint of 3 distinct objects: you, the racquet, and the ball. Now, simply use your muscles to move the racquet, not so much like a stroke, but as a flat object which you use to force the ball to go wherever you want it to go.

21

Hitting Drop Shots

The number one rule about drop shots is *not to try them on important points*. The notion that it is a crucial point will cause you either to play it too safe, resulting in an easy putaway for your opponent, or too good, resulting in a free point for your opponent. *The best time to attempt a drop shot from the baseline is early in your opponent's service game.* Unlike your own service game, you can afford to donate a point since you are not supposed to win that game anyways. You take your opponent by surprise and if it works, temporarily discombobulate him for the next point, providing an opening for you to break. Very often, he will want to respond with a drop shot of his own even at an inappropriate moment.

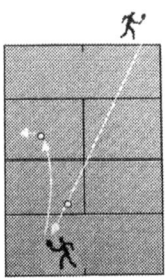

The easiest way to hit a drop shot is with a slice backhand off of your opponent's slice backhand. Make sure he is on his heels and not itching to chip your slice and come in. Once he gets used to you playing your slices deep crosscourt or down the line, he will not be leaning in looking to come to net. When you go to hit your drop shot, aim to hit it short and down the line. It should be like a short slice and not like a conventional drop shot per se. Hit the slice with extreme spin that makes the ball move to your left. Do not cut under it more or try to make the ball bounce back towards you; simply think of it like a normal slice but with more spin. This will cause the ball to run away from your opponent and if he gets to it, makes it difficult for him to put it away crosscourt. People try to hit a winner crosscourt anyways about 75% of the time and you should look for it.

Another factor to take into consideration when hitting drop shots is the wind. Never attempt drop shots with the wind at your back. It is just foolish. Conversely, if the wind is in your face, this is an excellent opportunity to hit drop shots. Make sure you get the ball over the net and then let the wind work for you.

22

Handling Drop Shots

As soon as you see the drop shot leave your opponent's racquet, get there as fast as you can. Do not try to time it so you get there just in the nick of time. Usually you will need ample time to adjust for unusual spin or unexpected wind. By catching the ball above the net and pounding it away, you will discourage your opponent from trying any more drop shots or make him try for too much next time.

The best place to hit the ball off of a drop shot is down the line. This ensures that even if he gets to it, he will not have a wide-open court to hit into. Most likely, your opponent will go for a crosscourt pass or lob off the next ball. You can already anticipate the crosscourt ball and put it away. Very few people are disciplined enough to play the ball back up the line. After hitting the drop shot, they are already frustrated that you got to it and are looking to hit a winner off the very next ball. The last thing they want to do is get into a cat and mouse game up the line.

Some players will hit the drop shot and close the net tightly. They are anticipating you to bunt the drop shot to their toes. *A good play is to bunt a flat lob over their heads.* Make sure you keep it on their backhand side. The lob is not something they are expecting and if they are close to the net, it will beat them. Do not hit the lob too high, just high enough to get over their heads. Do not be overly afraid of them smashing your face to smithereens with an overhead. It takes too much time to go from a volley mentality and put the racquet in the slot to hit an overhead off of your lob while the ball is on its way up. If the lob is low enough, it will come down quickly and they will have to let it bounce behind them.

After the lob beats them, get ready for their reply. Most people will just throw up a sky-high lob of their own, in which case you will have plenty of time. More advanced players will turn around to hit a normal groundstroke. These rarely pass a person at net, but when they do, 90% of the time it will be crosscourt. Be ready for a crosscourt shot if they do choose to hit a groundstroke.

23

The Volley Principles

Before you even consider yourself a volleyer, *you must have a great overhead.* Do not come to net if you cannot win nine out of ten points when someone gives you an overhead. Your entire strategy at net is based on the premise that your opponent cannot save himself with a mediocre lob. If you get nervous at the prospect of hitting an overhead, you might as well save yourself the energy and stay at the baseline. As soon as the lob goes up, back up, say "thank you" and hit that ball to kingdom come.

Although the overhead is a relatively easy shot, about two out of ten players chronically struggle hitting it. Remember, you do not have to involve your entire body like a normal stroke. Set your racquet high above your head and not resting on your shoulder. Focus on hitting the ball down into the court rather than outward in a more horizontal projectile. Your arm itself should have plenty of strength to put the ball away. By not relying on your body for power, you can hit overheads in almost any awkward position, even jumping in the air. This will also help you time the ball. Think of it like swatting a fly: you have very precise movement, can adjust quickly and are able to react instantaneously when using only your smaller muscles.

If your opponent throws up a high flat lob outdoors, you should always let it bounce. Give yourself enough room to gauge the ball and move your momentum back forwards into the overhead. It is very difficult to estimate the height of the ball against a sky background. Even if you feel certain about the timing, you will find that the ball is closer and falling faster than you thought. Your brain uses the relative sizes of objects to properly perceive their distance. Since the only objects to compare the ball to are infinitely distant clouds, your brain will overestimate the ball's height (this is the same optical illusion that makes the moon seem much farther away when it is high in the sky than when it is on the horizon).

If you are getting beat with a lot of lobs, you can fix this problem by changing the way your mind reacts to the lob. *When most players see a lob go up, their instinctive reaction is to try to reach up for it.* More often than not, the ball is way out of their reach. Only then do they start moving back. *Your first reaction should be to explode backwards and get behind the ball.* Only after you position yourself with your feet should you focus on your upper body and hitting the ball.

Half-volleys often cause players trouble. The main problem is the exquisite timing needed to swing at a moving, bouncing ball and make it go where you want it. If you hit it even slightly early or late, the ball will spray wide or pop up. *The trick is to eliminate two of the three independently moving factors.* As you are hitting your half-volley, pause your body's forward movement and don't swing at the ball with your racquet. Simply hold your racquet stationary behind the bounce, and let the ball hit off of your racquet. Since the half-volley is not a power shot, your opponent's pace will provide all the pace you need. When you watch Wimbledon, look for the pros to use this principle on their half-volleys. Even though their timing is very accurate, they just let the ball bounce off their racquet because they cannot adjust for the bad bounces quick enough. This slight change in your mindset will give you a more consistent half-volley.

There are a couple general rules you should remember when hitting volleys. Number one, unless you can put the ball away for sure crosscourt, *keep the ball down the line.* This ensures that you will be on balance in front of your opponent when he hits his next pass. Leaving the ball crosscourt turns it into a running game and lets him wrongfoot you as you race to cover the open court. Number two, *do not go for drop volleys off of low balls.* Your best bet is to keep low volleys deep. When your opponent dips a ball at your toes, his first reaction is to step into the court anticipating a short volley. It will be easier for him to cover a drop shot off a low volley because the ball has to travel up over the net and then back down again. A drop shot off a volley above the net will be more successful since you can drop it straight down over the net.

The basic strategy at net is to play as high percentage as possible. Keep your volleys and approaches low so that your opponent is in a defensive situation and has to hit up to you. Unless you keep the ball low, coming to net when they can hit passes down on you is almost suicide. Once you see he will not be able to hit a lob easily off your low approach, close tightly to the net. Make sure you shut the down the line pass completely. Do not let him beat you down the line. Many players will still try to squeeze the ball by you. You are in perfect position to slam these slower and high sitting passes. His only option now is crosscourt. By being so close to the net and because he has to hit up over the net, you are able to cut off most crosscourt rolls. If he tries to blast a ball at you, it will either go out or you can use his pace and block it down into the open court. Any hard hit ball around your chest will sail way out. The only way he can beat you is with a severe topspin angle. This is a very low percentage shot and you should welcome him to try it. Assuming that you can make a high percentage of your approach shots, this is an extremely advantageous position at net. Once in your spot, swarm all over your opponent, but be able to recognize a floater and pounce on it.

To simplify coming to net as much as possible, remember these few pointers. Stick your approach or first volley hard to make it difficult for your opponent to hit an offensive lob or create angle off his passing shot. Bank on the fact that he cannot lob or roll the ball by you and close the net tightly and quickly. Look to put the next ball away. If he barely gets to it, look for him to throw up a weak floater and pop it away. Don't forget, pace is more important on your initial approach than pure placement. Even if your shot is deep in the corner, you still leave him many options to pass you. *You do not want to be reacting to his passing shots.*

24

Simple Principles for Winning Doubles

Tactics flow from a superior position.
—**Bobby Fischer**

There are a few common mistakes that primarily singles players make playing doubles. When you are at net, do not turn your head and watch your partner hitting the ball at the baseline. If you get into a habit of doing this, one of these days the other team is going to poach and smash the ball in your face. You should be able to tell what is happening out of your peripheral vision and by your opponents' movement. Do not treat doubles like being responsible for half of the court. All too often, players just stand at net busy turning oxygen into carbon dioxide while the point is unfolding. Be aggressive. *A team with each player trying to win the point will always beat two players both trying not to lose it.*

Doubles is less about outright tennis skill and more about forcing your opponents' hand and executing your plays. A lesser talented team can win if it limits its opponents' options and plays smart. When you are serving, the point played off your first serve should be completely dictated by your team. Think of it like Tic Tac Toe. If you move first, you know you can win or at least tie every time. Getting most of your first serves in is crucial in controlling as many points as you can. Make sure your partner at net knows where the serve is going and with what spin. This will enable him to anticipate where the return will come and to pound it away.

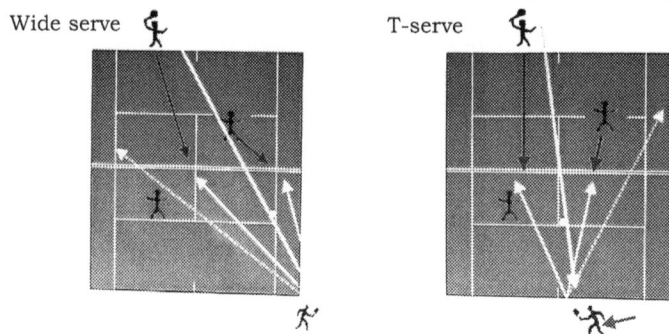

69

As one of my coaches, Ty Tucker, once said about doubles, "With a good serve, solid volleys and the right gameplan, you should never get broken." There are three basic plays when serving in doubles. For serves up the T, the netman should look to pick off balls in the middle of the court. He knows the returner will have a hard time hitting the ball back behind him. For body serves, the netman should close the net straight ahead because he knows the returner cannot get any angle or pace off the serve (see diagram). He should look for a floater that he can move to and put away. Wide serves are less useful in doubles and should only be used to keep the

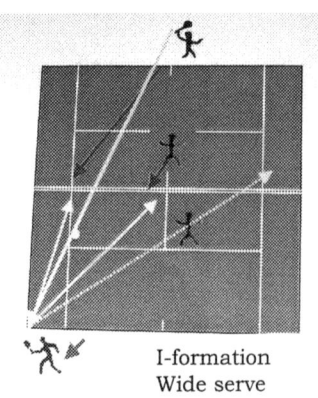
I-formation
Wide serve

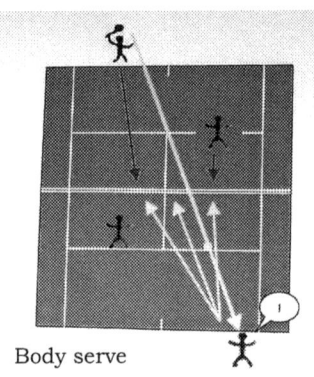
Body serve

returners honest. They open up the court and give the returner angles to work with. Once your opponents start hitting balls from the sidelines, they can use the lob and angles more effectively. If the ball is kept up the bulk of the court, your court coverage will not be compromised. When you do use the wide serve, the net man should cover the line and the server should serve and volley to the middle of the court (see diagram).

I-formation
T-serve

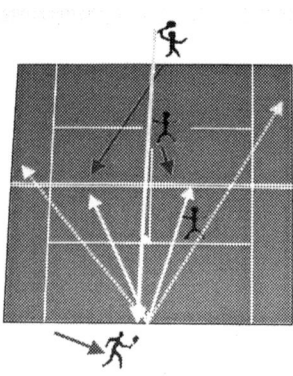

If your opponents are especially strong returners, you may have to use some smoke and mirrors to throw them out of their rhythm. One surprising play is the second serve poach. A smart returner will realize the value of seeing a second serve and not want to miss his return outright. Most likely, he is focused on getting the ball at the server's feet to make him play a difficult volley. If you poach late enough so that he cannot change his mind, you will pick off his return easily. Although this may seem risky, you have to take your opponent's frame of mind into account as well. The more important the point, the more conservative he will be off the return. Since your team is already at a disadvantage having to play off a second serve, you want the returner going for risky returns. If your opponent seems in a groove of blasting your first serves back for winners, try the I-formation (see above diagram). Have the server stand very close to the hash mark and the netman near the netstrap on the same side of the court as the server. Hit the serve out wide to the returner. The netman should stay in the middle of the court and the server should stay at the baseline and cover down the line. Force the returner to make his return down the line. The returner will not be able to hit the ball as hard because the net is higher and there is less court distance to work with.

You can also serve up the T in the I-formation. The server should serve and volley crosscourt while the netman looks to pick off the return. Anticipate that the returner will not be able to get the ball crosscourt (see diagram). These strategies should foil your opponents even if they have solid returns. Remember, once the returner gets the return past the server's partner and the server has to volley, the returning team is at an advantage. Off a low return, the returner's partner will always be looking to poach. It will be very difficult for the server to get a low volley by him.

      Once the point is extended past four shots, you should avoid getting stuck with one player at net and one player at the baseline. The one up one back formation is weak because it leaves the netman vulnerable to attack. If the other team gets the ball to the baseliner, they will close the net and pound putaways at the player at net. The best thing is to either retreat to the baseline or approach the net together. In the two back formation, fire balls up between your opponents to get them reaching for volleys. Always be ready for them hitting a drop shot. This is the only way they can hit winners against two baseliners back. Try to get them to hit a short volley. Isolate one volleyer by pounding the ball at him and approaching together. You and your partner should close the net to your spots, effectively cornering him (see below diagram). Try to hit your approach at his body so that he cannot get pace on his volley. Close quick enough so he cannot play cat and mouse to your toes. Usually, a volleyer will flinch off the approach and back up a little bit. This will give you space to put your volleys away.

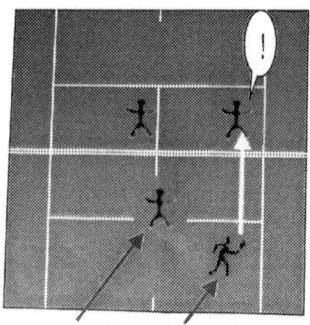

Many teams return serve with two back. As long as your volleys are proficient, the only reason to start off with both back is if the server's partner is hurting you with poaches and picking off volleys. In the two up situation, understanding who gets what ball is very important. This will prevent you from reaching for balls and leaving them short. The far player in doubles always covers the middle balls so that the near player never has to reach back to get it. The near player should just focus on the balls coming down his line. The far player should straddle the middle line and be ready to cover balls between them. Moving as a team, they follow the ball. The main idea is to play solid volleys back to the baseliners and not try to do anything special. You are in a positional advantage at this point and should wait for your opponents to take a risk and commit themselves. Look for an opportunity to put a volley away when your opponents are either stretched out or forced to play a half volley from the baseline. If your opponents are beginners, hold your ground and look for them to pop up a defensive lob. Make sure you communicate and know who is taking the overhead. If your opponents are more advanced, close tighter to the net and look for them to hit a normal groundstroke but with slightly less pace. Catch this ball above the net and put it away.

Perhaps the biggest factor in winning doubles, or any team sport for that matter, is achieving the right mindset. Contrary to common belief, the *most* valuable aspect of a team is not teamwork, but rather having individuals who want to win. Most successful teams are comprised of one or two stars who take it upon themselves to will their team to victory, while the rest of the team follows their lead. The successful team is *not* the team comprised of players who simply "cover their position" or "do their job." For these timid players, their first and foremost goal is to not screw up, rather than for the team to win. Likewise, it is detrimental for a team to have stars whose goal is to look good individually rather than to be on the winning team. The true star is one who takes it upon himself to win the game. He is the player who takes the fate of the team in his own hands, who knows that if he doesn't drive the team to victory, the team is not going to get there on its own. It is he who realizes that, hey, *I* want to win! *I* want us to win! And I can *make* it happen, not to just play and *see* if it'll happen. I can *force* both my and the team's destiny.

Perhaps the best way to start on this path, if you are stuck in the loser, "trying" mentality is to use your body to win, instead of your strokes – that if you hustle, you will throw your body, you will grind yourself to victory. I am fast enough, strong enough, and I have the <u>stamina</u> to win...that I will keep turning it up higher.

Think of it like facing a horde of men. On the other side is something you want so badly. These men will try to hold you back by physically grabbing your arms and legs. I will fight and scrap and claw my way through this horde, and even if they hold me, I will break their grasp...that if my mind is so inclined, I can make my body fight and fight and fight forever. Not even until my last ounce of strength, but rather until I achieve victory (note: the "until my last ounce of strength" mentality assumes the loser attitude). This is what makes "hustle" sports so great. If you have the basic strokes in tennis, you have all you need to fight for the win.

> Maradona is our maximum term of reference. No one embodies our essence better. No one bears our emblem more nobly. To no other, in the last twenty years, have we offered up so much passion. Argentina is Maradona, Maradona is Argentina.
> **—Gustavo Bernstein, Argentine Psychologist**

> God makes me play well. That is why I always make the sign of the cross when I walk out onto the field. I feel I would be betraying him if I didn't.

> When I wear the national team shirt, its sole contact with my skin makes it stand on end.
> **—Diego Maradona, the Greatest Soccer Player of the Century by vote of the people**

25

Sticking to the Plan

Jo: Listen. Danny. When you're out there. If it's not gonna happen – he's not gonna say it...don't go for it.
—**Demi Moore, <u>A Few Good Men</u>**

While there are many effective strategies out there, each with many permutations, ultimately you have to find one that works best for you. No one can simply give you the perfect formula to win. It is a process of evolution personalized by the countless experiences you gain over time. Without a set plan, you will find it difficult to win consistently. Every time you step onto the court, you will have to improvise and independently manufacture each point. You will never have a truly routine win. Simply having a plan is almost always better than having no plan whatsoever. Most low-caliber matches boil down to two players reacting to each other's reactions. Smart tennis is about having a system. Before you begin dreaming up any strategy, figure out what your strength is. Although many people list their serve as their number one stunner, you still need to build a strategy around a forehand, backhand or volley for points that get started. Once you decide on your big weapon, you need to discover a way to draw a ball on which you can use it. Similarly, you need to find ways to set up your set up shot. Pretty soon, you will develop a full-fledged combination attack. This is the manner in which players develop "multiple weapons," which is usually a misnomer since each weapon builds up to a final kill shot. Once a player hones his combination so well that each set up shot is independently dangerous, he has truly achieved multiple weapons. As you play, you should always try to apply your attack combination. No matter what ball is given to you, it should fit into some stage of your combination flow chart. Play every point according to your plan of attack and you will eventually tune the combination into a finely tuned weapon. By always having an idea of what direction you are trying to steer the point, you will never second guess your shot selection. For every ball and every situation, you will automatically know what to do. In addition, by always practicing your best combination and using it in every point, you can guarantee that you are always fighting with your biggest weapon and that your opponent will have to beat you at your most practiced skill.

Plug and Chug.
--Mr. Reeder, high school math teacher,
on using formulas

As with everything else, developing a combination is not about "figuring it out" or sitting at home with a dry erase board and drawing out plays. It is about having an awareness in practice and in matches to recognize patterns. It is about playing thousands of points and realizing what works in situ. Remember, the player armed with one coordinated system will always be better off than the player who randomly tries stuff from a bag of tricks.

> *Memorization is 75% organization. Think about books in a library – no librarian would be able to retrieve particular books if they were strewn lazily about the floor instead of being shelved properly. With the right organization, almost anyone can exhibit photographic-like memory. Formulating strategy is no different. Organize your game and from your system, you will always know what to use when and where according to the situation.*

Consider the following flowchart strategy:

1. Keep pounding backhands crosscourt until you draw a short down the line reply.
2. Pound forehand crosscourt, a la Figure-8 pattern, drawing another short down the line reply.
3. Take backhand crosscourt for second Figure-8 pattern.
4. Approach net if opponent is off-balance or reaching.
5. Hit first volley hard down the line.
6. Look to end point with overhead or putaway volley.

After mastering a sequence such as this, you can apply it to nearly every situation. If you have a neutral backhand, start at step 1. If you have a short forehand, start at step 2. No matter what ball is given to you, there will be no doubt in your mind what shot you should play. Every shot will have a purpose. Always try to set up your play. Only by playing hundreds of points will you be able to realize the best possible and most feasible sequence suited to your game.

Remember, do not look for the one shot knockout from a neutral position. Develop your pattern, play for position, then open up opportunities for winners.

26

Against the Big Server

The big server is often a difficult player to handle. This match will boil down to holds and breaks. If you can hold serve consistently, you will put pressure on his service games and not let him swing freely while up a break. Usually, a big server will have relatively impotent groundstrokes. However, do not let this lull you into just pushing your groundstrokes once you get the point started hoping he will miss. Because you are not putting any pressure on him, his vulnerable groundstrokes will not be exposed. *Continue to use your high percentage plays and make him come up with low percentage winners to beat you.* If you push, he will simply wait for a ball he really likes and take a chance on a winner. This is a bad situation for you because he has now taken fate into his own hands and eliminated you from the equation. His game is based on high risk, and he usually will make slightly more than he misses.

Another typical big server is the big bluff. Basically, his only true weapon is his serve. However, he feigns the rest of his game to intimidate his opponents with other shots. While his serve sets up other seemingly huge shots, these are not true weapons that can hurt you by themselves. *Do not be fooled by these players and think that you have to go for extraordinary risks yourself to beat him.* Realize what is blowing you off the court. Players can bluff their whole game because one shot sets up easy shots for everything else. This is true not only with the serve. Oftentimes, big servers are just hyped up pushers with a lot of smoke and mirrors. They may come to net to put pressure on you, but are only mediocre volleyers. Big servers rely on you being so impressed with their serve and their amazing putaways off easy volleys that you go for too much.

> *You must drain the swamp, or else you're just swatting mosquitoes.*
>
> **—Anonymous**

When returning the huge serve, keep the same ideas in mind. Usually, big servers have one bread and butter serve while all the others are simply diversionary. He uses these set up serves to keep you honest and prevent you from covering his favorite serve. Realize what serves are beating you. If you are getting blown off the court by his serve, simply move to the spot of his best serve and let him see you. Move around and change up the look, but let him know you have his big bomb covered. Now, make him beat you with his change-up serves. He will have to hit them with the pressure of knowing that he cannot still go to his ace in the hole. Oftentimes, his serve will break down. Without his first serve, he is a sitting duck, and you will be able to dismantle his game.

The number one thing to remember when playing a big server is that being able to return his first serve is not necessarily the key. It is more about how many points he has to start on his second serve. If you can win more than 60% of these points and if there are two or three games a set when he misses two out of his first three first serves, you have a good chance at winning.

27

Against the Netrusher

Defeating a netrusher requires more than honing your passing shots. You must understand the dynamics of the match. While most players become discouraged after getting passed several times, the true kamikaze netrusher will continue charging and make you keep beating him. He is betting that in the long run, you will not be able to come up with the goods time after time.

Holding serve is very important here. By winning your service games, you will not have to pass him for the entire match. All you need is to string together a few good passes for one break a set. To hold serve, playing high percentage off the baseline is crucial. You must win as many points as possible when he is not at net. If he is stuck at the baseline, apply pressure on his groundstrokes and do not let him approach. However, do not get drawn into taking low percentage risks. Netrushers may not have very forcing groundstrokes, but they often can be quick and competent counterpunchers.

Assuming he is able to chip and charge on your serve, he usually will not win more than 2 of these points a game. He relies on intimidation and on you donating the other two points. Make him hit volley putaways to win his points. Just because he is at net does not mean you have to pass him. The netrusher feeds off of errant passing shots and desperation lobs.

Another key factor is pressure. Focus on keeping the pressure off yourself by winning the first point or two in each game and always playing with a lead. The netrusher lets you decide the match, but puts as much pressure as possible on you. Take that pressure off yourself. Get up early and when he comes to net, envision yourself as having the advantage. He has put himself in a vulnerable position, and now you have an excellent opportunity to hit a winner by him.

Your approach to the match against a netrusher can decide the outcome. *It can be very intimidating to think that you will have to pass your opponent for the entire match, especially if your passing shots are not your strength. A better goal is to just string a few passing shots together in a row.* If you can do this on crucial points such as 0-15 or 30-30, these tiny opportunities will turn into a break of serve. Recognizing and capitalizing on these hidden openings is the name of the game against netrushers.

28

Against the Pusher

At all levels of the game, pushers are difficult opponents. They rely on playing extremely low risk tennis and letting you take high risks. There are basically two ways to defeat them. The first way is to approach the net and make them hit passing shots. Because passing shots are naturally higher risk than simply keeping groundstrokes in play, you are forcing the pushers out of their low risk comfort zone.

He fights hard, serves bad and volleys worse.
—**Adrian Bohane**

However, there are a couple potential problems with this strategy. Pushers are usually very quick and adept at hitting passing shots. In fact, they may encourage you to come to net. If you do not have superb volleys, pushers by their conservative nature will make you put away volleys before they miss a pass outright. Even if the pusher does not have great passing shots, by coming to net constantly, you are abandoning your own high percentage game plan. Putting the fate of the match at the mercy of anything but your forte is not high percentage tennis.

A better way to beat a pusher is by employing the crosscourt figure-8 pattern. Your opponent is playing low risk tennis and make him pay for it. Because the pusher is not hurting you with his shots, there is no rush or pressure on you to win the point. Only you can lose the point; he will not win it. *The basic idea is to punish the pusher for not doing anything with the ball by making him run.*

Do not get frustrated if you are not ending points. Even though you may feel like you're not winning the point, you are in a sense by depleting his energy. Since pushers hit the bulk of their balls in the middle of the court, you can run him around in an endless figure-8. When he starts getting tired, one of two things will happen. He could stick to his pusher gameplan until he cannot keep balls in play anymore. Or he will realize that all of his running is not paying off and abandon his primary strategy. Once he begins going for offense, the pusher is out of his element.

29

Against the Counterpuncher

At a slightly higher level of play than straightforward pushing is a style called counterpunching. In street fighting, a fighter is most vulnerable in the recoil after his attack. For a split second, he must open his guard to create offense. Tennis counterpunchers take advantage of this reality. Instead of imposing his own play onto you, he waits for you to make a move and then reacts to your game. He is quick and crafty, using your pace and angles to spot and create openings for himself. Seemingly every time you hit a forcing shot, he runs it down and comes up with an even more challenging reply. What seems to be his defense somehow turns into offense. Whatever you do, he seems to have an answer.

> *Baby, this is an island. If you don't bring it here, you won't find it here.*
> **—Harrison Ford in Six days, Seven nights**

The same approach that works with a pusher will not work against the counterpuncher. *The first thing you have to understand is that he cannot manufacture a point himself.* He relies on you initiating something for him to mount his game against. Assuming you are not such a superior player that you can manhandle him, you need to first establish your own defense. Counterpunchers often hit the ball short or up the middle of the court to tempt you. Foil this strategy by declining to attack and not compromising your own defensive court positioning. Hit the ball consistently back up the middle and show your opponent that you are patient enough to avoid all of their baits.

Eventually, counterpunchers become antsy and try to create their own offense. Because they are not used to this, they will usually attack wildly and attempt low percentage winners. Soon, they'll burn themselves out. Remember, do not give them anything to counter. Try to keep the point neutral and not let them play defense.

Carlos Fleming, one of my coaches, always emphasized the importance of having poise on the court. While there are many vital parts of poise such as composure, balance, and confidence, it takes on a whole new dimension in competition. Martial artists refer to it as Ring Generalship. A good fighter will always command the action of the fight. Even if he is not superior in skill, he can still prevail by determining how the fight is fought. Generalship is the difference between a player and a competitor. Oftentimes, it will be the only difference between winning and losing.

30

Against the Lefty

Assuming that you have gotten a handle on your lefty opponent's serve (see chapter on returning serve), the next task is defusing his tricky groundstroke game. The first thing to be aware of is that lefties love hitting the ball down the line, especially with the backhand. While he can slap winners crosscourt or down the line with the forehand, his basic backhand is down the line every time. Throughout their lives, lefties become accustomed to always keeping their primarily weaker shot to their opponent's primarily weaker shot. Some lefties may possess a sort of push angle crosscourt, but unless his last name is Rios, he probably has a lot of difficulty hitting a backhand deep crosscourt. This is especially true if they use two hands. When playing a lefty, you should definitely employ the crosscourt figure-8 pattern. In doing so, it is very helpful to have an effective crosscourt backhand. The play you need to prey on begins with a forceful crosscourt forehand. Your opponent will most likely try to rally a backhand down the line to your backhand. This is your money ball. Pound your backhand crosscourt immediately, looking to force a short response on the very next ball. Avoid engaging in a backhand crosscourt rally to his forehand. Unless you have a terrific backhand, he will have the upper hand. Unlike a righty's fairly flat backhand, a lefty's forehand spin will yank you off the court. Combat this by hitting your shots more up the middle of the court to give him less angle if you find yourself falling into this predicament. Look to set up your play over and over again.

In general, lefties prey on a society of 80% righty players. *Righties are accustomed to playing defense and creating offense towards another righty's backhand.* However, when they play a lefty, they find that their offense goes right towards their opponent's strength and they have difficulty finding the lefty's backhand. Usually, the righty spends the entire match trying to adjust his habits and hits his shots with only 75% of his normal ability since he has to come up seldom practiced shots. Instead of using the match to find your backhand down the line, simply employ your figure-8 crosscourt play. It will work whether you are playing a lefty or a right since your opponent can never change the geometry of the court. Once again, the match will boil down to who is the better player with more solid strokes. In fact, the play will turn it to your favor. Lefties who are used to hitting balls down the line against righties who struggle like fish out of the water to play the lefty's game, will in turn struggle to play your crosscourt game. They will instinctually revert back to hitting balls up the line and fall right into the wrong end of the figure-8.

Although there is usually no need to drastically change your serving plan against lefties, you should be aware of the slice serve out wide on the deuce side. It will be more effective against lefties because it swings out to their backhand. However, do not think that it will be cherry picking. Your serve may not have to be as well placed to cause them to stretch, but your follow up shot has to be better than against a righty. Instead of having to hit a backhand, the lefty will be able to track more balls down since he has the forehand to cover the open court. In addition, many lefties, over a lifetime of playing righties, have become adept at knifing backhand slices when pulled out wide. These are just several tips to use against lefties. The best way to handle lefties is to practice with as many of them as you can.

31

Stop Choking

There are many different culprits of choking and while losing your focus on the tiny tasks at hand is very prevalent, there is a more common and immediate cause to choking. Picture this scenario: You are poised to serve out the match at 5-4, 15-15 in the second set. After missing your first serve, a hint of nerves passes through your body and a troubling thought enters your mind. You realize that you've forgotten how you hit your second serve. Suddenly, the idea of hitting a second serve over the net and into the box seems more challenging than you've ever thought. Usually, you don't even give a second thought to your serve, but now, on the very verge of victory, your body stalls. In a state of panic and introspection, your mind prevents your subconscious from doing what it knows how to do. After double-faulting away your service game and proceeding to lose the match, you step onto the court the next day to practice your second serve. Much to your surprise, your second serve reappears as quickly as it had disappeared. What happened?

In order to prevent this kind of choking, you must understand the dynamics of learning your tennis strokes. When you first begin playing tennis, your body has no innate ability to hit the ball. Over time, you discover different ideas that seem to help you progress. They are usually special reminders you tell yourself each time you hit the ball. Gradually improving, you improve these key bits of advice for even more effective discoveries. Eventually, your shots become second nature and you are able to perform without consciously having to trigger your body. Although there is nothing wrong with relying on muscle memory, you should not completely switch to autopilot. Even if it seems like only a formality, repeat your trigger words to yourself as part of your routine. *Do not forget what conscious hints you used in the past to guide your body.* In crunch time, or if things should ever go awry, you will always be able to go back to your roots and manually override the malfunction.

Another force at work in choking is *the self-fulfilling prophecy.* When things start going south or the pressure begins to build, you begin to think of how you can choke the situation away. Indeed, you usually will choke once these thoughts gain momentum. However, you can use the same forces of self-fulfilling prophecy in your favor. Instead of recollecting your past choking incidents, imagine yourself as a clutch performer. *Imagine how everyone in the crowd knows you will pull it out.* Think of how John Elway and Michael Jordan felt when the game was on the line. They reveled in the clutch situation because they knew it was an opportunity to confirm their reputation as the Comeback Kid and Mr. Clutch.

> *Impress rather than just sliding by.* You get nervous when you try not to screw up. Don't just be good enough, be the best.

If your quandary with choking is not so much about playing in front of crowds, but rather involves nearing something you want very much, all you need to do is flip a switch in your mind. Instead of thinking how you could *lose* the trophy, think about how much you *want* it and how you're going to go out and get it. Look at it like you're one dog in a pack and someone threw a piece of meat into a field. You're going to fight tooth and claw to get it. The concept of "choking" is totally irrelevant – this isn't a performance, it's a forward charging fight to get something you want.

32

Strange Birds

In Case of Emergency, Read Chapter

While the following discussion may seem highly irregular to most readers, there are quite a few people for whom it may be useful. Because of the degree of distress various psychological conundrums can cause, especially in tennis, it is definitely worthwhile to include a few tips for solving them. However, if you are having no distressing mental problems in your game, it may be best to leave this chapter for another day. Read on at your own peril.

Tennis cannot be played purely on the subconscious level; it requires cues and direction from your conscious mind. Very often, players will cross the demarcation line between these two areas and hinder their own performance.

If you let your subconscious mind step over its boundary, that is, you stop thinking and play completely on instinct, you will lose the ability to avert disaster. This is similar to an out of control train. Without a conductor to temper and adjust the speed, the train will eventually either derail or stall. Once in a while, early in a match, you will feel "on" as if everything you hit falls in. As tempting as it is, do not simply go for all out winners. You must stick to your strategy. Even though many of your winners may go in, if the match becomes close, you will not have a solid base to fall back on. Because you are too nervous at this point to go for winners, you will have to resort to pushing. The best way to prevent your subconscious from completely taking over, both in matches and long term, is to always remember the certain thoughts that trigger your subconscious skills. For instance, "pound the ball crosscourt" or "ride the backhand slice" may evoke a cascade of desired subconscious responses. If you become too dependent on your autopilot, you may forget how to drive your game in times of emergency.

Just as tempering your autopilot is important, so too is keeping your conscious mind under control is vital to your game. Allowing your conscious mind stray into the subconscious is very dangerous territory. You risk altering your natural biomechanics. I refrain from elaborating more on the realm of the subconscious because as a reader, you already have the subconscious means within you. You just need the conscious cues to make them work. Think of it like a television. You do not need to know how the electrical circuits actually work, only how to turn it on and what buttons to press on the remote control. Once you open up the back of the set and start exploring, you risk damaging your television.

You get in trouble when you start breaking processes down into little pieces and having your mind send commands consciously for every step. It is best when you simply think or feel the end result and let your body fill in the middle. This is when you are at your most natural. While retaining simple instructions is useful, as in to prevent choking, there comes a point when you begin *questioning* minor components of the system that you can trigger a malignant trend of mental events.

There are a few important notes concerning the subject of thinking about tennis off the court. As a rule, I do not think about tennis (as it pertains to my strokes and techniques) off the court. While ideas about strategy are acceptable, though not recommended, hypothesizing about techniques are a definite no-no. Without an actual court to determine their worth, any technical ideas you have are just fantasy. Trying to fix problems off the court will ruin the mind-body connection you established on the court. Separate your time. Never take outside issues onto the court and never take tennis off the court. Remember, you do not have to be thinking about tennis in order to improve. Your subconscious needs a chance to consolidate the experiences it had on the court. There will be many practices when you feel stuck only to step on the court the next day and have that which seemed impossible a ten hours earlier come naturally.

Use the human intellect to draw connections and observe patterns between the experiences of reality. Dreaming up theories not based on experiences are arbitrary and simply an exercise in imagination. Guide your behavior based on concepts formed from actual experiences.

We do not have the creative capacity to generate completely new ideas. All of our so-called "insights" are simply new connections between existing points. Experience provides us with those points. Only then can we learn and improve by drawing connections. Trying to fabricate our own points is mere folly. You cannot plot the points yourself and draw the lines. Dreaming up new theories and techniques off the court are based on mind simulated experiences and all of your groundless lines of insight will disappear when plotted in real life. Do not become enamored with your own creativity.

Many players watch instructional tennis videos and pro tennis on television. These are decent sources to glean strategical tips, but do not try to imitate their more detailed techniques. For instance, you should notice what volleys a serve and volleyer looks for after different serves, but copying the angle of someone's wrist on their forehand is too much. Each person's body is a little different and moves in unique way. To manually force your body to imitate someone else's exact posture will only hinder your own natural fluidity. If you find yourself analyzing a pro's motion in slow motion, you know you have gone too far. Imitating a better player's overall form is often helpful, but make sure it is only a general likeness. Left alone, your body will move in the manner most efficient for your physique. In addition, be careful if you watch videos of yourself play. You already have a certain feel for yourself that manifests itself in what you see on video. If you see yourself play too much, it may start a bad trend. The next time you step onto the court, you may be overly conscious of your own motion.

Ironically, this can lead to you imitating your own motion. This "tail wagging the dog" phenomenon is definitely a contraindication of analyzing yourself on tape.

Oftentimes, teaching pros will use videos of top tennis players to bolster their own instruction. Using a slow motion clip, they usually point to a minute detail of the player's stroke and claim that tiny technique is the secret to mastering the shot. While it is irrefutably evident that the player on video does perform that movement, it is highly unlikely that the player actually is aware of it. Instead of consciously trying to copy every subconscious movement of the top player, you need to find the right conscious cue he uses to trigger the effective subconscious cascade.

There is one cardinal rule in preventing psychological problems in tennis. Do not perform a repetitive action too many times. While repetition can be helpful, there is a point, past the point of diminishing return, when repetition actually becomes harmful. One example is continually rallying balls up the middle of the court for hours at end. After a while, your mind will start wandering and slowly become idle. Without new external input, your mind, always hungry for stimulus, will begin looking for it from within. Once your mind starts observing itself, you may find yourself quickly entangled in mental knots.

One specific problem that is worth mentioning is having trouble switching grips. When done naturally and subconsciously, it is a smooth transition from shot to shot. On the contrary, it is a quite impossible task for the conscious mind to keep up with. In the case that your conscious mind refuses to let your subconscious mind do its job and it cannot figure out how to do it itself, here are some general pointers. One, don't try to anticipate what shot the other guy is going to hit or where he's going to hit it, and start switching your grip to the stroke you think you'll need. Two, when your opponent hits it and you have to react to it, don't react by frantically trying to switch to that stroke's grip. Three, do not switch grips before your opponent hits the ball – if you remember instances where it was as if you were "waiting" with your forehand since you knew exactly where he was going to hit the ball, understand that you are not literally (physically) waiting with your forehand. It is only your mind that has visualized the shot and mentally prepared itself to make the physical switch to the forehand, thus making it an almost instantaneous adjustment when your opponent actually hits it there. The trick to switching your grip (and this only applies to players who currently have the problem) is to visualize your next shot as the ball is still traveling towards your opponent (i.e., "I am going to pound it crosscourt – no matter where he hits it back). After your opponent makes contact and as the ball is traveling towards your court, just keep thinking about your end goal (of pounding it crosscourt) and let your body fill in the rest (i.e., moving to the ball, switching to the appropriate grip, etc.). As you regain your natural comfort, you can relax your mental discipline and not have to decide where you're going to hit the ball until after your opponent has hit it.

Obsessive thoughts can become quite bothersome if not controlled properly. An important key is realizing their origin. Many times, obsessive thoughts are the product of the over-valuation of things. Notice that young children are not inclined to have obsessions. They do not over-valuate things because they simply are not aware of the consequences. However, overzealous parents and other influences can scare children into having obsessions. Once people realize that they could lose something that they hold valuable or irreplaceable, they become obsessed with protecting it. Ironically, this usually leads to exactly what they are trying to prevent. You must tell yourself: *I will not over-value everything which I could potentially lose.* And if indeed it is priceless, *instead of trying to make sure I won't lose it, I will try to make it better.* Remember, things are either moving forward or backward – never stationary. Read on.

For those of you who do not understand what plagues many people, consider this: it is not so much the fear of the thought itself, but rather the fear of the thought that you can't get rid of the thought. It is easy to put thoughts into your head, but how do you get thoughts out of your head? Initially, people have an unflappable sense of mind over body – that one can will one's body to do or not do anything. However, what about mind over mind? Sure, one can resist impulse and temptation, but what about conscious vs. subconscious? One way to get a thought out of your head is to just replace it with different one. However, what if the troublesome thought comes up every time you need to do a certain regularly necessary action? What if the thought was previously subconscious, but now has become conscious? Or even, what if the action itself used to be subconscious, and your conscious does not know how to do it, but will not get out of the way? Well, you have quite a quandary on your hands! How do you get the horse back into the barn?

If this sounds like your problem, then the solution is quite simple. However, you must truly understand the spirit in which you go about it. Realizing it will be like an epiphany, a moment of "A-ha!" You will instantly know that you are headed the right direction (in contrast with many of the other "textbook" methods you may have tried, which make it seem like you are only covering up the problem).

What you need to do is focus on the final task rather than on the obstructive thought. Tell yourself: I am going to do my final task even if this thought is in the way (I accept that it is there) – I'll fight through it to do the final task, *but I am not fighting the thought itself.* I am simply trying to do the final task. For instance, if I have to play soccer, but one of my hands is tied behind my back, I am going to focus on winning the soccer game (fighting through my handicap, but not focusing on it). A good analogy is wearing glasses. If, for instance, I have a smudge on my glasses, it can be very annoying if I focus (either with my eyes or my mind) on the smudge. However, if I focus on things beyond my own glasses, the smudge disappears and is no longer a hindrance.

> *Look with your mind beyond the obsession – you do not need to solve or clear the "near" issues in order for them to go away.*

If you have serious trouble with your game because you have started to "think about your shots," don't try to figure out what you used to do that made it work – simply accept your shot as it is right now, and try to improve it from there. You don't need to search for your old groove; in trying to perfect the shot you have, you'll make it better, often finding inadvertently or surpassing your old shot. Do not worry about losing it forever or moving in a different direction – every path of improvement eventually leads to the same destination. As you consciously work to solidify a shot, your body will subconsciously optimize its movement.

33

Enter the Zone

Because so much emphasis, perhaps unnecessarily, has been placed on what sports psychologists describe as "the zone," I would be remiss in not including it in a tennis book. Before we examine the famous zone, let us deal with its diametric opposite, self-awareness. The evolution of self-awareness in apes is very interesting and can shed light on what it takes to find your zone. Famous anthropologist, Richard Leakey writes,

> Players of social chess must be constantly alert, on the lookout for potential advantage, watchful for unexpected disadvantage [. . .] The challenge for individuals in primate societies is to be able to predict the behaviors of others. [. . .] If, for example, individuals were able to monitor their own behavior rather than operate like computer-like automatons, [. . .] by extrapolation, they might then be able to predict the behavior of others under the same circumstances. This monitoring ability, which Humphrey calls the Inner Eye, is one definition of consciousness, and it would confer considerable evolutionary advantage in those individuals that possessed it [. . .] As the Inner Eye became ever more observant, inexorably there would emerge a real sense of self, a reflective consciousness, an Inner I.

It has been demonstrated that only the chimpanzee can recognize a mirror image as itself. Except for these certain primates with self-consciousness, all other animals are permanently in the zone. They can only see and react to the world and outside stimulus, but have no introspective notion that they exist as individuals and cannot comprehend themselves from an outside point of view. While self-awareness confers an advantage limited only to humans, it presents a unique problem for us that proves to be an unwelcome scourge in sports and performance.

It is fairly common for the human mind to interfere with the body's instinctual guidance, resulting in disastrously sub par levels of performance. However, from horse-racing to dog-fighting, this problem never occurs with animals because, by lack of higher mental power or imagination, they are forever and inescapably in the zone. In order to find the zone, you must lose your self-awareness, that is, forget that "you" exist as an entity in this world. All there is is the outside world, the sensations of sight, smell and sound. As "you" disappears, you become the court itself.

Many people define the zone as the ability to stay in the present. While this is true to a certain extent, it is actually slightly, yet significantly incorrect. On a superficial level, you are indeed in a zone if you can set aside your plans for a celebratory dance and concentrate on the match at hand. However, for more sophisticated players, there is a more focused zone you need to be in. Think about your mind, if that is possible, during your everyday routine. You will notice that it operates a split second ahead of your body's actions, always sending the next signal to your muscles just as your body carries out the previous task. In essence, your mind is in "prescient time" while your body is in "current time." This is the modus operandi for the zone. When you freeze up in a match, the moment you become self-aware, your mind loses its split second prescience and starts sensing your own body's movement. From current time, it cannot send advance impulses to your muscles and you lose the sensation of "in the zone" omnipotence. Without the mind to guide it, the body falls behind and stalls.

While your conscious mind may be able to briefly observe current time and let your mental autopilot command prescient time, your conscious mind must eventually return to the wheel. In order to stay in the zone, you must always give your conscious mind cues to think ahead. Certain phrase words that capture your plan for the immediate future will trigger a forward charging, instead of backward looking, consciousness. "Pound the ball crosscourt" and "attack the ball with your feet" are both examples of slightly prescient commands. Remember, when staying in the zone, keep your mind pressing forward and your body will follow every whim exactly, ultimately disappearing. Your thoughts will become action.

34

The World of Cheating

Because tennis players call their own lines, cheating is an unfortunate part of the game. The best way to approach this is through the Prisoner's Dilemma. Ideally, your opponent and you should cooperate and both refrain from cheating. This creates the best environment for playing tennis. However, there are personality types that try to take advantage of the situation. They will trick you into cooperating and then cheat you on an important point. If you turn out to be the sucker, this is the worst possible outcome for you in the Prisoner's Dilemma. You should accept the fact that you are playing a non-cooperator and make the best of the situation.

> *If he made his calls any tighter, there wouldn't be any court left to hit into.*
> **—Dave Schilling**

It has been shown that the best strategy in the Prisoner's Dilemma is Tit for Tat. Mirror his previous action. If your opponent cooperates, cooperate. If he cheats, cheat. Always remember what he did last time, and do not stray from your Tit for Tat policy. As one of my coaches once said, "If you are playing a cheater and you do not cheat back, you are only cheating yourself." Even though Tit for Tat is a good rule of thumb, you have to treat each scenario appropriately.

The easiest way to handle cheating is by calling an umpire to your match. However, this may not always be satisfactory. Be sure to return the favor before you call the line judge. If the hook is especially egregious and cheating him back will not reverse the damage, take action. Change the score in the game so that he will not be able to claim his stolen point. Disagree with him until you have to go back and replay the entire game. While you are arguing, make sure a line judge is present so that he will not be tempted to one up you and change the entire set score. This is an extreme measure. If your opponent is making suspicious but not blatantly close calls, question him very intently. He may be simply floating a trial balloon to test your reaction. Oftentimes, he will feel guilty or self-conscious and give you calls later. Be wary of players that seem magnanimous or complimentary at the beginning of the match. They are dangerous appeasers and usually try to soften you up for a later hook.

Jimmy Dugan (to his player): *Are you crying? Are you crying? There's no crying, there's no crying in baseball.*
Umpire: *Perhaps you chastised her too vehemently. Good rule of thumb, treat each of these girls as you would treat your mother.*
(Brief Silence)
Jimmy Dugan: *Did I ever tell you, you look like a p[otato] with a little hat on?*

**—Tom Hanks as Jimmy Dugan in
A League of Their Own**

It is not uncommon for line judges to be swayed by the players. Although I do not advocate playing mind games with the poor officials, sometimes you have to engage in a little psychology to offset your opponent's attempts. If you question the right calls with enough passion, the line judge will feel obligated to overrule in your favor eventually. However, this is a double-edged sword. Feeling his duty to act as a fair arbitrator, he will try to create equality by returning the favor to your opponent. Do not get in the habit of harassing the line judge. He will become biased against you. His ego will persuade him not to give you an overrule lest he feel like he succumbed to your constant barking and intimidation.

I once knew a player who was especially adept at manipulating line judges. During the early stages of the match, he would create the impression that he was a sort of line judge himself. To exhibit his objectivity, he would call balls out and then correct himself in a bout of seeming generosity. Not only would he call out balls out, but he would also signal balls in when his opponent hit a winner. In his subconscious mind, the real line judge would begin to see this player as a second judge, someone who lent support to his calls. Later in the match, when this player wanted an overrule, he immediately ran to the line judge with his hand signaling an "in" sign. As he nodded his head, he would state, "that ball was good, right?" This plays on several levels.

Naturally, people's first reaction is to agree. It is human instinct to avoid confrontation. Notice that this tricky player does not ask the line judge, he states. He extends his hand and nods his head, both positive signs. Unless the line judge is absolutely sure about the call, this ploy usually works like a charm. If your opponent is pulling stunts like this, work to get your offsetting opinion in the judge's head as well. Do not let the line judge forget that your opponent is a subjective player with his own intentions in mind. If you cannot see where the ball is landing on the other side of the court, do not be afraid to question your opponent anyway. Very often, your feel of the ball coming off your strings is a pretty accurate judge whether your shot was in or out. Do not give him the benefit of the doubt over your own court sense.

Because people can do and say anything just to make you feel good, you cannot judge them by their words or even actions. You must observe them and judge what kind of person they really are.

Earlier I mentioned that the typical tennis hook is the Prisoner's Dilemma Cheater. However, there is another, less iniquitous personality type that can fall into the cheating habit. Sometimes, very relentless and inspired juniors who value the praise and approval of people away from the tournament will succumb to temptation. Because their target audience sees only the final result of the match on paper, the junior will sacrifice the respect of his peers for the approval of outsiders.

Cheating is a bad habit, and it is a slippery slope. Once you start calling balls out, you realize that you can win points that you previously lost. When you give yourself the option of cheating, you are faced with the choice of having the point or not. Instead of your opponent winning it, you feel as if you are simply and needlessly giving it away. You must reverse this thought process as soon as possible. The easiest way is to simply call the balls exactly as you see them. Never be generous in practice either. This will cause you to hesitate in a real match. Make it a reflex and do not think. You must not establish a gradient in your mind of "in-ness" and "out-ness."

> *Competition is hell. Winning is heaven. True athletes are driven by a love of the prize, not the process (truly uncertain competition is fun only in retrospect). Those who cheat are cowards – they seek winning, but cannot stomach competition.*

In the long run, it is never worth it to cheat. The joy of victory lies in the respect and admiration of others. When you cheat, your reputation will be tainted. All of your opponents, assuming that you are a cheater, will ascribe to the Tit for Tat strategy and cheat. This will make all of your matches unpleasant and you will never be able to enjoy the environment of a mutually cooperative match.

35

In Front of Crowds

A common scenario you will face with the biggest of your opportunities is playing in front of a crowd. Very few people seem truly comfortable performing in front of an audience. Although these rare individuals are often described as natural-born performers, there is nothing innate about their talent. It all stems from their conceived approval, which in turn breeds actual approval. As a young child, they were always exposed to center stage. Whether they were really outstanding or simply in front of a supportive audience, they received plenty of praise. After years of reinforcement, their impregnable belief in themselves validated itself through the self-fulfilling prophecy.

Confidence in front of a crowd has nothing to do with actual skill or even confidence in that skill. It just boils down to knowing that audiences love you. The next time you have to make a public speech, don't just shoot for normalcy, hoping that people won't notice your deficiencies and point you out. The next time you play tennis in front of a crowd, do not be nervous. Aim to impress them. Know that they are not judging you, but rather already approve of you. Make it your encore, not your audition. The crowd will be disappointed if you treated them to anything less. Show them how it's done. You love it.

36

The Lure of the Big Game

> *Gatsby believed in the green light, the orgastic future that year by year recedes before us. It eluded us then, but that's no matter—tomorrow we will run faster, stretch our arms farther...*
>
> *Then one fine morning—so we beat on, boats against the current, borne back ceaselessly into the past.*
> —**F. Scott Fitzgerald, <u>The Great Gatsby</u>**

Every player, at a certain point in his game's development, will feel that he is not playing a big enough game. Perhaps he has one favorite shot that he can hit with impunity. It is natural to think that if he could bludgeon all of his strokes like that one, his game would skyrocket. Not only that, but winning would be so much easier as well. No longer would he have to grind out every point. He could use his impressive arsenal of weapons to blow opponents out of the water. This is the Lure of the Big Game.

Oftentimes, a player will fall for it when he is at an all time high in his career. After a big win, when his confidence is high, he tries to take an even bigger bite out of the pie in the sky. Modeling his game after superior players, he changes his strokes for the game of the future. At first, his new strokes feel good. However, after the novelty of these techniques wear off, he realizes that they are not as good as his old ones. If only he listened to the old maxim, "If it ain't broke, don't fix it."

Most players turn back at this juncture, quickly reverting to their old game and regaining their winning ways. Some players keep on pressing. One may think that it is gamblers who would keep pressing. Nonetheless, the gambler types are too addicted to winning and return to what they remembered to work. Interestingly enough, the players of a more conservative inclination press onward with the big game. Their mentality all too often is that they would rather sacrifice and take some lumps now for the higher reward of success later. Unable to cut his losses as sunk cost, this player continues to search for that "secret" technique that will revolutionize his game. Unhappy with his old-fashioned coach, he opts for more ambitious direction. Perhaps he even chooses to walk the path alone.

> *If you live in the past, you die a little every day.*
> —**Juliette Lewis, <u>Cape Fear</u>**

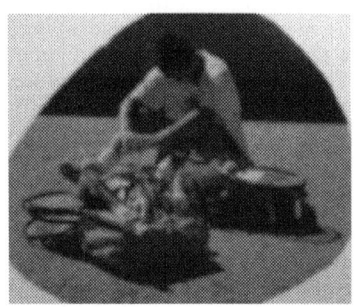

Months go by and he wanders farther and farther astray. For him, it is never a matter of making up his mind. Though he knows his destination, he is without location. Slowly, he loses the fortitude and desire to compete, wanting only to find the game to hit people off the court. Hoping to have an epiphany one day, he spends numerous hours in deep thought, mulling over books and tapes. There are many long drives home, even longer nights, and very short matches. His game and ranking begin to slide. People tell him that the pace of tennis has passed him by. If only he had his old game to show them. Injuries crop up and exacerbate the situation. Friends console him by accusing his bum elbow or hurt knee. This offers him no solace. Caught between the elusive new game and the shell of his old game, he knows the real culprit was the day he started looking for the Big Game.

> *He managed to sneak by you*
> **—Dave Schilling, on losing 6-0 6-0**

Some players quit at this point, a very ignominious end to a career so promising. A player who at his peak one day, began a slow but unstoppable decline. A player whose very desire of the pie in the sky was the reason for his demise. The same dying aspiration that enabled him to sacrifice hours of enjoyment for hours working on the court caused him to sacrifice his own game for a phantom image. He was the dog in Aesop's fable that dropped the steak in his mouth for a reflection of the same steak in the river. There is no rock bottom to this sad story. With the clock past midnight, there will be no quick return to glory. Losses will compound upon losses until he yields all hope of a last second save.

> *Yesterday is gone. Tomorrow never comes. 'But today,' the A.A. says, 'today, I will not take a drink. I may be tempted to take a drink tomorrow – and perhaps I will. But tomorrow is something to worry about when it comes.' The A.A. does not cling to the hope of being able to drink normally again.*
> **—44 Questions, Alcoholics Anonymous**

Amongst white water rafting aficionados, there is a well-known river phenomenon called 'holes with keeper hydraulics' or in short, 'reversals.' These river spots occur after large physical obstructions such as rocks and logs where the water will cause a falling flow that pulls surface water back upstream and hold its contents, including ejected passengers, indefinitely. Because the threat of drowning in one of these reversals is very real, rafting guides always tell their passengers how to extricate themselves from such a quandary. The trick is actually counterintuitive. If you fight the current and try to surface, you will never escape the keeper hydraulics. You must curl tightly into a ball, increasing your density and sink to the bottom of the river where the swirling water will release its hold. Now, you can simply let the nature of the river carry you downstream by itself.

Once the broken player releases all hope of recapturing his past, he can start anew. He will be a beginner again, forgetting all of the adulterous lures that bastardized a once great game.

> *Hold!....Hold!.....Hold!.....*
> —**William Wallace,** as the English cavalry charged towards the Scottish front line, <u>Braveheart</u>.

If there is only one piece of advice you take from this book, let this be it. Do not get greedy with improvement. This idea is not so much about "sticking with the basics," an oft quoted piece of advice that sounds very unattractively small minded and does not feed the fire of more ambitious players. You must be patient and not try to force an opportunity where there really isn't an opening. Too many people do not have the staying power or the endurance of mind to see things through to the end. While everyone around you starts to panic, lose their cool and change their game, stick to your guns and hold the line. Remember, no shot alone will defeat your opponent. No shot will do your dirty work for you. You will always need to enter the ring and defeat him yourself.

> <u>The Lure of the Big Game in a Nutshell</u>
>
> *The Victim: A late starter, but rapidly improving player.*
> *The Setting: Getting ready to break into the top ranks and having a taste of success.*
> *The Signs: None. At the current rate, has potential to surpass peers.*
> *The Instigating Event: A close loss to a very highly ranked player.*
> *The Thought Process: "I am so close, but without a bigger game, I will never reach the next level. However, when I get that bigger game, I will truly blow by these chumps."*
> *The Subsequent Actions: Scrap current strategy even though it had yielded success, brought improvement and had no sign of slowing down. Leave current coach for one that espouses the bigger game (or go with no coach at all).*
> *Conventional Wisdom Interlude: "That's the problem with players that haven't won their entire life – they get a few*

wins and start thinking they're going to break through all of a sudden."

The Problems: Gradual, but definite decline – increased losses interspersed with a few moderate wins. The player loses interest in working hard in practice and lessons – "I need to work on my strokes, not my conditioning."

The Bottom: Lopsided losses to previously close competitors. Embarrassing struggles and close losses against lowly ranked players. Loss of name recognition and "aura" against opponents

The Attempted Recovery: The player tries to use old form / strategy to no avail – it doesn't seem to work as well as it did in the past. Can neither recapture old game nor find a new big game. Several months at this level, the player ponders quitting.

Cure: Accept present game for what it is and treat it as ground zero, a new starting point. Accept the permanent loss of the old, previously successful game – do not try or hope to recapture it. Forget the dream of the big game and do not get side-tracked trying to find it. Start anew and improve the present game, most likely on a different path than your original one, though down the road, they may reconvene. The key is to think: work on present, not recapture old or find new. Learn as if you are a beginner.

Prevention in the first place: Do not tear down a successful strategy / game. If it does not work as well against players ranked higher than you, keep exposing and applying it to them. Soon, it will yield a little bit of success; add this to your game and use it to gain more success and to pry your way into the next level.

37

The Evolutionary Way of Learning

The setting: Millions of years ago, A bunch of apes are sitting around in the desert. Suddenly, giant black monolithic slab arises from the ground. Its perfectly right angled edges and smooth metallic sheen are completely incongruent with the pristine beauty of a pre-human world. With much caution and trepidation, the apes approach the slab and run their hands across its surface.

The next day, one of the apes is playing idly with a bone. As if endowed with intelligence beyond his pre-hominid brain by the previous day's experience, he realizes that he can use a large bone to break smaller bones. It is a moment of epiphany and he throws the bone high into the air in exultation – and in pure cinematic symbolism of evolution and intelligence, the bone transforms into a futuristic space shuttle orbiting the earth.

—2001: A Space Odyssey

Through the continual process of mutation and natural selection, every individual organism possesses many adaptations perfectly suited to its environment. Just as Darwin outlined these forces as evolution, so too can you apply them to tennis as a way of learning and improving.

School is not so much for learning math, science or history. It is where you learn how to learn.

—Frank Ng

Every organism's ultimate goal of survival and replication is what drives evolution. Likewise, set your goal to winning as much as possible. In nature, organisms do not actively try to change their behavior to enhance their survival. They cling for their life to what is familiar to them and has been proven to work. Over time, slight mutations cause variation in the species' behavior and characteristics. Subject to the pressures of natural selection, these alterations are either incorporated or instantly moded out.

In training, you should always focus on what you know works and try to solidify those principles. The more you practice, the better your body is able to adjust and subconsciously evolve to maximize your biomechanics. As you are playing, you may serendipitously realize that something you did, a spontaneous "mutant" action, will work slightly better than what you usually do. If this new alteration proves itself against the pressure of winning, you can incorporate this beneficial addition into your stroke. However, it is important to remember that you cannot plan or design your improvement; it will come when it comes, and only when you are actively solidifying your existing game. Work hard on what you have, know the direction you want to go, and you will become a very evolved and advanced tennis creature.

> Keep in mind that analogies are only useful in explaining something. They cannot be used to support a point or prove something because you can always find an analogy to show anything.

The general idea of the evolutionary way of learning is to accumulate rather than exchange. Never give up what you know to work and have spent a long time solidifying for the unsubstantiated promise of something better. A true improvement should never require you to "change" your shot; it should be an addition to what you already have. It should also immediately enhance your game. Although this seems to be an illogical and impatient approach to learning, it is necessary in tennis. There are simply too many theories that sound good on paper but lead nowhere for you to base your game on one person's speculation "for the long run." Beware of the initial good feeling associated with any change, but always demand evidence from yourself of immediate improvement before making any adjustments.

> Improvement will come through perfecting what you have and trying to win against higher levels of competition – do not seek change in an effort to improve.

If your ultimate goal is to turn your humble forehand into a deadly weapon, do not rehaul what you already have. Make your humble forehand the best it can be and eventually, it will build on itself. Each level is the stepping stone for the next. Only if you had a very major deficiency in your stroke would you need to completely reconstruct it.

Many players wonder "Should I try to win or should I focus on playing good tennis?" *You should always try to win. Contrary to popular opinion, just trying to play good tennis is not the key to the "winning in the long run."* The general tennis community has a fondness of designating a certain style of play as "the right way" or as having the characteristic of "good tennis". This style more often than not involves going for winners, attacking at all cost, and looking professional. Do not feel pressured to adjust your style or strokes just to conform to the norm. Listen to the standard truisms of good technique with a grain of salt. Ninety-nine percent of the definition of good tennis is set forth by armchair experts who react ex post facto to players they see on TV. The fact of the matter is that most successful pros do not play conventional tennis. Only after they appear on the scene do people include their style of play as acceptable good tennis.

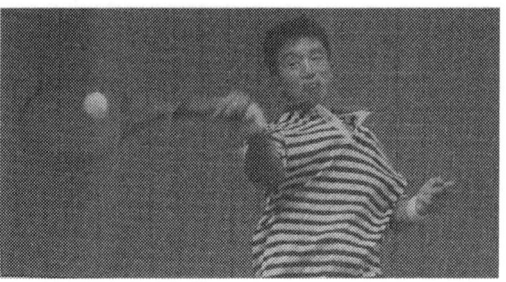

Whenever you step onto the court, winning should be your foremost goal. The top pros did not get to where they are by trying to play "good" tennis and sacrificing winning. They did not wake up one day and find themselves beating people they used to lose to. They did not develop into a winning machine by discovering one trick that revolutionized their game. Ninety-nine percent of the pros you see on TV were winners their whole life. Chances are, they were top five in 12 and under, 14 and under, 16 and under and 18 and under. Common to all of them is an intense need to win. This drive placed tremendous natural selection on their game and they have accumulated hundreds of effective principles, all geared specifically at winning. Through long practices, their strokes evolved to what you see them as today. What appears as a unified whole can be deconstructed into many subtle parts. To think that you can get to where they are simply by imitating the appearance of their game and not going through the process of trying to win is wishful thinking. What differentiates a top 100 pro from a top 500 pro is not so much their level of skill, but rather in the number of winning principles each has gathered over their career. Remember, it is not good tennis unless it is winning tennis.

Improvement and Change are not synonymous. You do not have to change in order to get better. Improving by making what you have better is not glamorous, but works.

Many players fall into the trap of thinking they can be their own coach. Their logic goes something like this: "If I can always make my coach's new techniques work, why can't I just study the game and think of new techniques myself?" There is a fundamental difference between getting instruction from a coach you believe in and getting it from yourself. When the coach gives you instruction, you naturally try to make it work. Surprisingly, it is more important that you believe in the coach's advice than whether the advice is actually good or bad. As soon as you start trying to win, the evolutionary process is set into motion and your body begins to improve on the stroke. On the other hand, when you coach yourself and come up with your own techniques, your approach has more of a "trying it out" and "wait for it to work" attitude than a "trying to make it work" attitude. Instead of the evolutionary process, you invoke a shotgun experimental process². Remember, improvement is not the result of trading up for better and better shots; it is from continual adding and accumulation to the same stroke. Always aim to perfect your existing game in an effort to win. Discoveries and improvement will come when you pit it against the challenge of stronger players. Your game will advance like evolution – not as one or two giant leaps for man-kind, but rather as tiny, yet significant steps forward, each arising dependently upon the prior step, forming a wondrously interdependent and almost impossibly complex creation.

Intelligence is a form of Evolution

A common mistake is changing your game in order to beat players ranked much higher than you. If you are #60, do not start going for winners because that is the only way you think you can beat players in the top 10. Focus on what is needed to beat players between #30 to #80. Once you are ranked in the top 20, then you can focus on what is needed to win at that level. Most likely, the top 10 players will not seem as good as they once had and options less drastic than simply going for winners will be available to you at that point. Consider making progress in tennis like finding the cure for cancer. *Instead of trying to cure it all at once, look for treatments that can extend patients' lives by one day or one month, then keep building it up until you get there.*

Remember, set your sights high, but set your plan according to where you are now. This is especially important for juniors – they should not mix up having high goals with skipping steps and jumping ahead.

Improvement will come through the evolution of your strokes against the natural selection of winning, and not through the conscious creation of techniques and theories.

Perhaps the best way of understanding the mental and physical evolution that a high level player goes through in improving his game is to listen what the players have to say for themselves. One thing to notice, however, is that the thought processes and feelings that the players have to achieve the improvement are not simply the mechanical changes that outside observers notice, and sometimes try to replicate. If anything, it should be the internal concept and feel that people should emulate because the motion itself is largely a product of an individual's build and only represents the shell of the more important inner sense. From an interview with Ichiro Suzuki, arguably one of the best pure hitters in baseball today:

As Ichiro stood in his customary spot on the first-base side of the cage during batting practice, a thought popped into his mind: What if he made a subtle change to his stance?

---

² One telltale sign of experimenting is getting rusty very quickly and needing an unusually long time to warm up before your strokes feel good. The "rust" is actually the good feeling generated by a stroke's "newness" wearing off.

As he often does while waiting in that grassy patch, Ichiro made a few exaggerated golf-like swings. Liking the way they felt, he used the slightly altered stance in the cage. A bit more intrigued, he used the stance in that day's game...beginning July 1st, he went on a 21 game hitting streak.

To Ichiro, batting largely is about capturing a unique but essential feeling. "What I gained with the change was simply a feeling, so it's difficult to describe...I describe myself as the kind of batter who tracks the ball on a line, so how quickly I can enter that plane is crucial. As the ball is released from the pitcher's hand and comes toward me, first my eyes and then my entire body enters the line formed by this motion. My bat is the last part that enters the line."

To the casual eye, there are three main differences in his appearance in the batter's box. His front foot is farther off the plate, his stance is narrower, and the bat is in a more reclined position as opposed to pointing skyward. The changes are more complex than simple cosmetics.

—**Brad Lefton, Sporting News**

38

Troubleshoot Your Progress: Find, Don't Seek

> Govinda: *I am indeed old, but I have never ceased seeking. I will never cease seeking. That seems to be my destiny. It seems to me that you also have sought. Will you talk to me a little about it, my friend?*
> Siddharta: *What could I say to you that would be of value, except that perhaps you seek too much, that as a result of your seeking you cannot find.*
> Govinda: *How is that?*
> Siddharta: *When someone is seeking, it happens quite easily that he only sees the thing that he is seeking; that he is unable to find anything, unable to absorb anything, because he is only thinking of the thing he is seeking, because he has a goal, because he is obsessed with his goal. Seeking means: to have a goal; but finding means: to be free, to be receptive, to have no goal. You, O worthy one, are perhaps indeed a seeker, for in striving towards your goal, you do not see many things that are under your nose.*
>
> —**Hermann Hesse, <u>Siddharta</u>**

If you seem not to be improving despite patience and hard work, ask yourself a few questions. When you practice, are you always trying to reinforce the shots as they are? Let improvement happen by itself. Trying to experiment with new techniques and becoming disgusted when they do not pan out will only lead to fruitless hours on the court. You are not giving yourself a chance to improve because you are too busy thinking.

A common practice mistake is frequently changing your strokes. New motions feel good and you can gain an immediate high from them. Your muscles are designed to detect changes in movement pathways. As your newfound strokes lose their novelty, you will find that they lose their appeal. Do not fall for the temptation and into the trap of always changing your techniques. There is a learning curve and you have to give your body a chance to optimize itself after the initial change wears off. No technique is the answer in itself. You must let your body adjust and make the technique work for you.

At a certain level in your career, you will inevitably develop an itch to make radical changes in your game, thinking it will make you better. <u>At first, a newly conceived shot will work surprisingly well</u>. However, once it moves past the experimental phase and you have to rely on it as your breadwinner, its initial efficacy and appeal will quickly fade (always take this into account when deciding to change your stroke). As a rule, never clown around with brand new ideas "just to see if it works." While you clown around, you destroy the feel of your normal shot; experiment too much and you may never be able to get it back. Most likely, you are talented enough to make any funky motion work a few times, but that is no indication that it is actually better than your old and proven shot. Understand that each stroke in your game is not self-encapsulated. The way you hit your forehand is closely linked to your backhand preparation. Changing one stroke may have unexpected implications. With improvement, the operative words are "hone" and "notice" rather than "experiment" or "figure out." It is tempting to totally revamp a stroke, but "new shots" are never made this way. Making small changes entails that your stroke is never truly new, simply a growth of your old shot.

> *Think big, think positive. Never show any sign of weakness. Always go for the throat. Buy low, sell high. Fear...that's the other guy's problem.*
> **—Dan Aykroyd in Trading Places**

If you are ever unsatisfied with your progress or feel disillusioned about the entire process, take this into consideration. No matter what level of the game you play whether it is junior, college, or professional, most players are fairly equal in skill. *While the difference between levels are not very large, there are many players at each level.* If you improve a little bit, you will pass a lot of people. Do not think that you have to make huge strides to achieve relative progress. However, the converse is true as well. Never take your ranking and status for granted. If you slide a little bit or even tread water for too long, there are hordes of players that will race ahead of you. Once you fall behind, you may never be able to claw your way back. Do not be fooled into thinking that players much better or much worse than you.

Perhaps the best way to look at improvement is through the eyes of an investor in the stock market. Investment analysts Koch and DeSalvo write,

> *The single most important thing you can do for yourself as an investor is to develop a long-term perspective. This will inoculate you against the persuasive pitches to buy the latest hot investment and prevent you from selling based on bits of news and rumors.*

Indeed, once you pick good stocks for your portfolio, you must have faith and let them work for you. If you keep buying and selling, you lose tax and commission each time, never letting interest and gains accumulate. Similarly, if you invest in a stroke, stay with it and let your improvement build upon itself. As hard as it may be, you must purge yourself of the temptation to always change. So before you set off questing, remember, there is a certain fascination in choosing the proverbial "road not taken," but it takes infinitely more will, faith and perseverance to stay the course and prove yourself amongst the throngs of others. Your true strength lies within you. It does not reside with any coach or stroke you may have. If you are ever in doubt, win. Try to win as hard as you can and you will not go wrong.

If you ever encounter a seemingly unsolvable problem, or if it seems like every time you solve one problem, another pops up, take this advice. Do not focus on your problems as if they are a worsening of your previous self and avoid the mentality of "if I could only rid myself of this one problem and return to how I was." Accept your present level, no matter what it is, and focus on improving it. This approach will always help you succeed.

Improvement in Tennis

Most players have one shot that comes natural to them. It is not only their best weapon, but is also the Rock of Gibraltar against which the rest of their game leans. It is a shot that is always two levels above the rest of their game – a shot capable of hanging with better overall players.

Use this shot to improve the rest of your game. If it is your backhand, all improvement will run through your backhand; use it to win and let the rest of your game supplement it. Your backhand will drag the rest of your game forward. It is your hook to the next level. Do not fall for the trap, "If only I could hit my forehand as well as my backhand." It is too difficult in tennis to move a broad front forward.

39

Lost Strokes

Once upon a time, there was a self-made Millionaire. He worked hard his entire life, saving 80 cents of every dollar and living the Horatio Alger rags-to-riches dream. One day, while he was passing through Las Vegas, he began thinking about gambling. He thought, "I already have so much money; one big gamble and I can be a billionaire. I could work my entire life and never make a billion dollars. I would rather go for the glory than to toil forever and not accomplish anything extraordinary." With that, the Millionaire started gambling. On some days, he won, but most of the time, he ended up with a little less than when he started. After the Millionaire lost most of his fortune, he became desperate and was concerned only with recuperating his original million. Soon, the Millionaire had to pick up a small job on the side. However, every time he looked at his measly paycheck, he became thoroughly depressed and thought back to his old million. After every payday, the Millionaire went back to the casino to try to turn his new earnings into the old million. Nevertheless, each day of gambling brought him closer and closer to bankruptcy. One day, he did reach rock bottom, but this did not stop him. He started drilling. The Millionaire took out loans and sold all of his belongings. Finally, he was broken, not only financially, but spiritually as well. Sitting on a park bench one day, he looked down and saw a penny on the ground. The Millionaire picked it up and held it in his hand. It felt dirty to him and he was about to throw it away in frustration and disgust when a distant memory ran through his mind. He took a second look at the penny. Suddenly he started to feel better. Smiling, the Millionaire said, "Penny, I accept you and will keep you as my own. As much as I hate you, you are all I have. I am giving up on my old million, and I will work with you." With that, the Millionaire took his penny and left Vegas and his old million behind. For many years, he worked for his money and saved 90 cents of every dollar. He never ended up reaching a billion dollars, but he made many millions along the way.

Ask any tennis player and he or she will tell you a similar story. Whether they lost the stroke themselves or know someone who lost their stroke, it will always be the same. Some people can come to terms with their loss, accept the present situation and begin the improvement process anew. Others cannot, sinking further and further into despair until they give up. Ironically, the moment they give up on their old stroke, they are one step closer to the solution and need only to rekindle the fighting spirit within them.

The ages of 17-20 were hard times in my life....but let me start at the beginning.

I started tennis when I was 11, and I was at the bottom of the tennis ladder – years behind the other players who had started at 7 or 8. However, over the next 5 years, I made tremendous progress and eventually surpassed them. My improvement was rapid – I ended up #1 in the Midwest section. A short 6 years after starting tennis, I found myself in the third set with the eventual national champion on center court. It crossed my mind that I was not very far from the very top. I felt nothing could stop my ascent.

However, I began having problems with my strokes. I remember the exact moment when it all started. Lazily letting a ball jam my backhand, I immediately felt a tingle run down my spine. From this one miss hit, I knew something was wrong. A process of deterioration had been set in motion. It would transpire over the next 4 years, leading me into a suffocating depth worse than any nightmare.

My backhand, which had always been my go-to shot, felt different. I began over-analyzing it until I completely lost it. I questioned all of my strokes; I left my coach. It was a precipitous decline. I sank to new lows every time I stepped onto the court. I lost to players I had beaten years before. I had lost everything I achieved, not only my ranking, but my game as well. They were dark times and hard to reckon with.

On many occasions, I tried to summon some courage, some fighting spirit, some work ethic; I tried gimmicks and accessories. I reverted back to old habits in desperate attempts to rekindle my old feel. Something – anything to put my foot down to stop the slide and turn the ship around. However, it was not happening. I could not stop my game from falling apart. In fact, it had already fallen apart long ago. My mind was in pieces. I could not even make contact – I was missing the ball completely. I went from a worthy opponent to nothing but a running joke, a literal buffoon on the tennis court. If you know who Ian Baker Finch is, you know part of the story.

I spent four years bloodied, but unbowed. I refused to take a knee. But finally, I could withstand it no more. I had to let go. I gave up on my game. I gave up on trying to get it all back. I tried too many 11th hour saves – the night practices before big matches, the early morning hits, the consultation of stroke doctors – they all failed. I had sat in many places before a broken man, but always before, I retained some glimmer of hope. But not this time, there was none. I thought it was all over.

Several years have passed since that day, yet I still remember it as the moment that everything turned around. It was dusk on a cold November evening and I found myself sitting in the middle of the football field at Brecksville-Broadview Heights High School. Having reached a level lower than rock bottom, I gave myself two choices: I could either quit tennis completely or continue to play, but give up on the backhand I loved so dearly. As I pondered these equally sad options, I found something that would change the course of my life. Lying in the grass was a chain bracelet. It was very unusual because the links were in the shape of tiny footprints, each connected toe to heel. As I picked it up, the clasp of the bracelet fell open and the circle of footprints straightened out. I had asked for my backhand, but received a gift much more valuable. I now knew what I had to do. I accepted the ruins that were my backhand and made up my mind to always charge forward, never trying to reclaim the past or hold onto the present.

As I stood up that day, I breathed the cool, refreshing winter air and looked into the clear blue sky. I felt that a vice had been removed from my chest. There wasn't that dying corpse that I could not save rotting away inside of me anymore. I felt newly born – a man without history, without repute, without a name to reclaim.

And so, I started anew. I was a beginner. I trained along new paths – I did not seek to find or retrace my footsteps. I learned with unjaded eyes. I was a new sprout – fresh, and growing for the first time. It was the greatest feeling in the world.

> *Kneel...On your knees!*
> *Be without fear in the face of your enemies*
> *Be brave and upright that God may love thee*
> *Speak the truth even if it leads to your death*
> *Save God and the Helpless, and do no wrong*
> *That is your oath...[Slap!]...And that, is so you remember it.*
> *Rise a Knight!*
>
> Priest: *Does making a man a knight make him a better fighter?*
> Orlando Bloom: *Yes.*
>
> – **Kingdom of Heaven**

40

Keys to Junior Tennis

> *The 2 keys to junior tennis are not losing to players you're not supposed to by building a strong base, and being able to recognize when you're playing a stronger player and stepping up your game by 15%.*
> **—Ty Tucker**

Learning tennis correctly as a junior is crucial. When you are a child, your mind is very fertile. If the right seeds are not planted, it will take a long time to undo bad habits. The way your body conceptualizes tennis is formulated in the early stages as a beginner. Unless this is done properly, certain strokes may elude you for the rest of your career. In addition, there is no time to waste if you want to succeed in the junior ranks. The rate of junior development is at a breakneck pace. Kids will improve simply by getting older and stronger. You must accelerate your improvement to the second derivative in order to get ahead. If you spend any time spinning your wheels, you will be run over by a stampede of your peers. However, carefully nurtured, your game will be light years more mature than those of your misguided competitors.

> *While you're sleeping, I'll be training. While you're eating, I'll be running. While you're resting, I'll be lifting. I want it.*
> **—Anonymous**

The Suzuki method of learning violin is a perfect example of the great opportunity to acquire a skill during childhood. Immersed into a passive musical environment during his formative years, a child learns the delicate nuances of pitch and tone, and develops an "ear" for the music. The impressions and feelings gained through this osmosis become part of his nature and accelerate his future progress. Like violin, tennis training at an early age has great potential for creating a child prodigy. It is important, should you choose to enroll your young child into tennis, to monitor his training. Unlike violin, there is no common proven school or established method of teaching tennis.

> *You either get the notes right, or you get the rhythm right. If not, just try not to make any noise.*
> **—Orchestra Conductor M. Kessler**

There are several key aspects to making sure your junior training is as efficient as possible. The first stroke a child should learn to hit is the backhand. Do not let your child rely on a forehand and slide by without a backhand. Most likely, the two-handed backhand will be the most natural shot for him to use to keep the ball in play. Developing a solid backhand as a kid will carry you for your entire career and always give you an advantage over other players who never learned it and always struggle to hit it.

The reason the two handed backhand is so good to learn as a child is because you are tiny and weak compared to the racquet and ball. You must rely on using both arms and your whole body to generate pace and control the ball. This will necessarily engender good technique. If you wait until you grow older and stronger to learn the backhand, you are prone to just arm the backhand and to only use your smaller muscles. Adults with tennis elbow is a perfect example. Instead of involving their entire body, they feel more natural merely using their forearm to hit the ball. There is no need to give your child extensive technical advice. Simply let him play with an adult racquet and encourage him to use both hands to hit the ball. Naturally, his body will adjust itself and the stroke will evolve perfectly. A terrific model of the two-handed backhand is Monica Seles. Even though she is a fully-grown adult, her stroke epitomizes that of a youngster. This affords her tremendous power and control indicative of maximizing all of her strength.

> *There has been better talent and better minds that have come before you and did not make it. Even if you have Top 100 talent, it is still a long shot – there are many pitfalls along the way.*
>
> **—Ty Tucker**

When first learning the two handed backhand, try to hit the ball crosscourt every time. This will naturally teach you to use your entire body. If you start off with down the line shots, you will develop a tendency to arm the ball and ingrain a poor conception of the backhand. After you master the crosscourt backhand, you do not have to alter it for hitting the ball down the line. You can conceptualize the down the line shot as simply a less severe crosscourt backhand. There is no need to hit it later, to extend more with the arms, to have extra turn in your shoulders or any other commonly suggested advice. All you have to do is not hit your backhand as far crosscourt. Indeed, unless you are hitting it inside-out, every backhand, including down the line, is still crosscourt relative to you.

> There are plenty of horticulturists out there who like to grow plants, but it is a special person who finds unique enjoyment in germinating seeds.
>
> **—Jane Ellison**

Another key component of junior development is speed training. Running agility drills will help smooth the often awkward transition from a child-like frame into an adult body. Done frequent enough, it will avert those years of unnatural movement associated with sudden growth spurts. Instead of letting speed gradually grow into your body, force your body to become accustomed to speed. It is a popular myth that some people are born slow while all of their speedy compatriots are naturally gifted. While there are a few exceptions, seemingly innate speed can be attributed primarily to early exposure to quick movement. If you train your fast twitch muscles and reflexes as a child, it will become ingrained and second nature in your body. As you grow older, even with a few years of indolence, rapid movement will never seem foreign and you will know what it takes to move fast.

> Sometimes a player will have a weak shot that simply seems wrong, or "looks weird" in a bad way. More often than not, the problem is not in the motion per se, but rather in the player's whole conception of the stroke. It runs deeper than just reformulating a new understanding because oftentimes the player started hitting the shot this way since day one. It is similar to the question, how can one comprehend the color blue if he has never seen blue, or how can one explain sound if he has never heard? The correct conception is not something that can necessarily be taught from the get-go. If a child, due to his body structure, mind-body coordination or previous athletic experience feels most natural, or rather, comprehends hitting the ball a certain way, there is little that a coach can do to explain or train him to do otherwise. Motions and even mechanics can be altered, but an inherent deficiency due to that player's signature lack of comprehension will always be evident. Perhaps the natural emergence on day one of the optimal body conception to hit a shot is the origin of what people call Talent.

One important aspect of junior improvement is always pushing the envelope in practice. It is always ideal to compete with slightly better and older players. By exposing your game to a more rigorous natural selection, it will evolve faster and become accustomed to a superior level. Since anything but the most effective plays will not work, you discover quickly what wins at a higher level. Each day in practice, you have to rise to the occasion. By always chasing a goal, you never become complacent. It is easy to lose your drive if you always feel safe ahead of the pack.

> *Many in the crowd, thinking that Connors had too much to overcome, headed for the exits. Soon down 4-1 in the third set, there seemed to be little doubt about the outcome...BUT! – with the clock past midnight, Connors summoned his legendary fighting spirit (running backhand passing shot), and Patrick McEnroe found it hard to handle (crowd goes wild).....*
>
> *Connors arrived at what seemed impossible, just two hours earlier: match point. It was an opportunity he would not let slip away (Connors wins the match). 'Patrick let me in the match, and this crowd won it for me, this crowd here.' And so, Connors lived, to fight another day. Many will claim to have been there, only wishing that they were.*
> **—Al Trautwig, commentator for**
> **US Open 1991: An Open for All Ages**

While practice is about biting off more than you can finish, competition is a different story. You should not compete in a higher age group until you have proven your domination in your own. You must learn how to play under the pressure of being expected to win. It teaches you mental toughness. By always being the underdog in a higher age group, you never have to put your ego on the line. With everything to gain and nothing to lose, it is like playing Vegas blackjack using Monopoly money. When it comes time to reverse the roles to be the favorite, you may find yourself faltering and looking for excuses. In addition, do not forget that winning is a habit. Expecting to win as a self-fulfilling prophecy is often half the battle. The more you win, the less readily you will accept losing. You must learn how to guard against the bad loss before shooting for the up win.

> *You can't just jump up the ladder – you've gotta touch every rung.*
> **—Ty Tucker**

A lot of people will look at a better player and remark, "He doesn't really do anything special." However, understand that all of his strokes are very solid such that none are disproportionately better than the rest. Hence, he does not need to rely on any one of them to be his breadwinner. Additionally, he does not need to do anything special to win. As the better player, it is not his job to prove his game to his opponent, but rather quite the opposite. His opponent must take the chances, and if he is successful, then and only then, will the better player feel compelled to raise his game and take chances of his own. Think of it like a medieval battle. An attacking army must prove itself a threat before a walled city will send its troops out to meet them on the battlefield. Otherwise, the walled defenders will simply fight from behind the safety of the walls and let the unworthy enemies throw themselves to their demise trying to scale the city.

41

Finding a Coach

> *Happy families are all alike; every unhappy family is unhappy in its own way.*
> —**Leo Tolstoy, <u>Anna Karenina</u>**

Choosing the right coach may be the single most significant factor in determining your child's success. The number one rule is that parent coaches do not work for teenagers. While this may work in childhood, once your kid becomes an adolescent, it is a recipe for long arguments and disaster. Father-son pairings are rare. By nature, teens are seeking independence. They want to have a separate voice of their own and do not want to simply be an automaton of their parent. Being able to claim their accomplishments as their own is part of finding an identity in the eyes of others. Oftentimes, teens will disagree with their parents just to avoid feeling dutiful. Remember, miscreant teens do the "wrong" things, not because of anything inherently appealing about doing them, but because they were done under the teen's own initiative. It is worth noting that the apprehension of being dutiful usually does not apply to juniors instructed by an outside coach.

> *Most of the time I don't have much fun.. The rest of the time I don't have any fun at all.*
> —**Woody Allen**

For the preteen player, the parent coach presents another problem. It is very important for the child to have a relationship to his parents separate from tennis. A parent coach's instruction may be perceived by the child as an admonishment of a personal flaw in his overall character. Your child's game must remain the purview of a coach and let the family serve as a respite and safehouse of support and love. This arrangement will protect against emotional breakdowns and allow your child pursue tennis without the pressure of winning his parents' approval.

Many parents who have not played tennis themselves tend to oversimplify the game and reduce its complexity into the tip of the iceberg they see as spectators. Do not assume that just because you have watched many hours of tennis and have heard the advice of many coaches, you know what is going on and can administer the right ounce of cure at the right time. Simply memorizing and repeating what coaches have said in the past is not good enough; a true teacher's words come from experience. On a side note, feeding balls is not simple – it requires placement and timing. If you are not a player yourself, do everyone a favor and don't feed to your kid; it will cause more harm than good.

In general, the best policy is to always encourage your child to succeed during these often turbulent and angst-ridden years. Unless something is obviously astray or deviant in your child's actions or unless he asks for council, parents should not try to change their child's tennis.

> One problem in juniors is the natural teenage urge to idolize and emulate heroes (not bad in itself) which causes them to model their game after players on TV, forgoing simpler, yet effective winning strategies and failing to learn the discipline it takes to win day in and day out.

If tennis improvement is important to you and your child, finding a suitable coach will take valuable research. Do not simply drop your kid off with the local country club pro and expect him to be winning college scholarships by the end of the summer. There are several things you must look for in a good coach. If you are not an experienced player yourself, it may be difficult to wade through a lot of the malarkey floating around out there. Make sure the coach cares. A lot of tennis pros simply go through the motions after teaching hundreds of lessons during the week. This kind of apathy is not what will get your kid to the next level. Although there are plenty of teaching pros that are diligent and give their best every time, your best bet is to find someone who only gives private lessons on the side. Most often, these are ex-players who have found jobs in other fields or in different avenues of tennis and only teach players with promise. You can be sure that he has interest in your child's improvement and well being since he is taking time out of his day to teach your child. Since he does not rely on students for a living, he will promote independent thought because he does not have the financial pressure to create coach-dependent players. You should never rely on a coach to prop you up. Always remember, professional coaches will tend to peddle "the perfect game" or "the right way to play" lest you ask yourself, what are we paying him for? In the same vein, most coaches will feel obligated, whenever you make a mistake, to offer some bit of correction, albeit superfluous, as a sort of band-aid to make you feel better about missing. This tendency, unfortunately, is oftentimes counterproductive as you focus more on incorporating every little piece of advice rather than developing an overall system based on a few permanent principles. Although the quick fix is the cathartic answer, true improvement comes gradually over the course of many drills. Most discoveries are the result of success plus observation, not failure plus change.

> Vince: *Have you ever run into something you just couldn't comprehend?*
> T.A. Brian: *If you don't understand something, it just means you don't have the right textbook.*

When looking into a coach, make sure he has playing credentials to his name. Unless he was able to apply his knowledge himself, he will not be able to impart his largely hypothetical advice effectively. He is just a "parrot of other men's thinking" (Emerson 53). By merely reiterating what he has heard, he passes along the word and spectator knowledge, but not the wisdom and actual facility.

> *Unless you truly understand how everything in the system fits together and fully internalize the underlying concepts, all of the techniques and pointers will be superficial and seemingly random (i.e., not natural outgrowths of the foundation); you will not be employing them with the right mindset.*

Be aware of Ockham's Razor! Some tennis coaches will try to push their pet theory, though unfounded in any experience, onto their students under the coattail of other legitimate advice. Do not become a coach's guinea pig, no matter how illustrious he happens to be.

> Hypothesis: *The planets move around the sun in an elliptical path due to the will of powerful aliens.*
> Conclusion: *The planets move around the sun in an elliptical path; therefore, powerful aliens must exist.*
> Occam's Razor: *"Pluralitas non est poneda sine necessitate"*
> —*Entities should not be multiplied unnecessarily*

A brief word needs to be said about temptation and change. Oftentimes, devious coaches and other people in society will plant seeds in your mind as temptations for change. Realize that how you consider their offer will mold your feelings and ultimate decision. Given a proposition, you can either think, "I want it, but I'm going to stop myself" or "I don't want it, but he is trying to pull me in." The former is a self-fulfilling prophecy and inexorably leads to you doing it, whereas the latter is a safer attitude. Either way, make sure you know which side you are approaching the coin from and in the end, you will be able to better judge your own reasoning. In addition, avoid arguments such as "you'll always regret not having gone for it" and "you never take any chances" to guide your choices. There are plenty of instances, though you may not remember, where more cautious decision making averted debacle. Always follow your best judgment of the situation and do not factor in unrelated previous events.

> *At the very top level, its about the kid, not the coach. The best thing the coach can do is provide solid guidance – nothing fancy – and get out of the way. The kid is the great player; the coach cannot create the great player.*

Get opinions from other players who were contemporaries of your coach in his playing days. Many boastful coaches will try to associate themselves with better players by dropping names. If a coach touts all the players he has "made" as evidence of his genius, be wary. Very few great players are the result of just one coach. Chances are, he is taking more credit than he is due; these players were probably good before they even met him. A truly good coach knows that the development of a player lies more in the player himself than the coach.

> *For the 1st lesson, I want you to play over every column of Modern Chess Openings, including the footnotes. And for the next lesson, I want you to do it again.*
> **—Bobby Fischer (advice to his biographer, Frank Brady, who had asked for chess lessons)**

Do your homework before you choose a coach and it will be well worth it. Be sure to always observe your child's lessons. Make sure the coach is attentive and his instruction makes common sense. Even if you are not sure about something, do not think the coach is some sort of illuminati. However, do not scrutinize him overzealously. Be sure he is still conducting the lesson for your child's benefit and not just for your approval.

> *Everyone wants some magic from a coach – well, I've got some magic – it's called work your butt off for 6 hrs a day for 8 months and see where it gets you!*
> **—Anonymous**

Adolescence is a time of lofty ambitions and dreams. While this quixotic fervor is undoubtedly a sign of great things to come, make sure your child does not lose a grip on reality. Since he is looking for independence and new creation, he is very susceptible to being brainwashed by a coach. Feeding him high sounding ideas, this coach may lead your child astray. Avoid coaches with delusions of grandeur; if anything, he should be more grounded and should serve as the voice of conservatism. Beware of coaches who brag about having secrets behind shots and a revolutionary theory. It is tempting for your child to believe that he finally found someone who can lead him to glory. That is just fantasy. There is no little tree gnome with a magic potion, no Yoda with secret forces (see next chapter on Cults). The charlatans always feed you what you want to hear. He is only doing you a disservice. Make sure it makes sense to you. Remind your child that unlike Star Wars and Lord of the Rings, real life is about hard work and keeping your nose to the grindstone.

> *The making of pictures is a stern discipline. One may 'write around' a subject where one is not quite sure of the details, but with brush in hand before the drawing board, one must be precise and realistic. The white paper before the artist demands the truth.*
> **—Frank H. Netter, MD**

Most junior players are 1st generation tennis players, that is, their parents are not experienced in the game. Thus, it is relatively easy for a 20-year veteran of the coaching circuit to smooth-talk even the most discriminating parents. However, there is one method that parents can use to fairly accurately decide whether or not to stick with a coach. That gauge is winning. If the coach's changes are truly improvements, then they should help you win in tournaments. Although it is tempting, do not base your judgment on the promise of future winning, how well the shots look in drills, or how many practice games you can win (many coaches will keep promising future success...all the way until it is time for the kid to leave for college!). While good teaching will make sense, do not assume everything that is logical is good teaching; there are simply too many good sounding theories floating around out there. Remember, be addicted to winning and your progress will be a relentless march forward.

> Kaffee: *Would you put him on the stand?*
> Sam: *No.*
> Kaffee: *You think my father would've?*
> Sam: *Not in a million years...But here's the thing -- and there's really no way of getting around this – neither Lionel Kaffee nor Sam Weinberg are lead counsel for the defense in the matter of U.S. versus Dawson and Downey. So there's only one question: What would you do?*
> **—Tom Cruise, Kevin Pollak and Demi Moore,**
> **A Few Good Men**

A good coach does not have to give you a blueprint for success. Do not become too dependent on him. You must avoid seeing yourself simply as a memory box, robotically programmed to carry out his techniques. Imbibe his advice and discover their effectiveness for you. Learning to win and sailing the sea is your task. While the coach gives advice, strategical and technical, you should only use these ideas as a compass and direction, ultimately making your own discoveries in trying to learn your coach's lessons. Do not fall into the two crutches, "If I follow this person's advice exactly, everything will be perfect" and "If something is not working, it must be because I failed to follow some part of his advice." No coach's advice will be the end-all and be-all. A coach should tell you what worked for him as a player and is a good general rule to abide by, but in the end, you have to make it work for you. This usually involves going beyond their teaching and developing additional permutations that fit it to you and your game. If you cannot do this, you are nothing but a made-man, a vessel of other people's thoughts, a conglomerate of various pieces of advice lacking integrational insight, forever unable to surpass the quality of the input you were given. Remember, learning is not merely the process of acquiring knowledge; it is the creation of knowledge as well. Far too many players become expert-happy and their quest for knowledge simply becomes a quest for the next best expert. They know only the advice and instruction of others, and lack the confidence borne of knowledge based on personal experience.

> *If I have seen further, it is by standing on the shoulders of giants.*
> **—Isaac Newton**

When confronted with a decision or problem, you may ask yourself, "What would person X do in this situation?" What you don't understand is that a true teacher's ideas are not medallions to drape around your neck or images to keep burnt in your memory. Instead of a liferaft to which you must cling, the teacher gives you a stepping stool so that you may see for yourself. He offers you food, nourishment of knowledge, to be eaten and digested, to be assimilated into your own life-force. You cannot take the food and save it forever and ever – it is useless in this manner. You will not be able to bring it out when it is needed as if it were some magic talisman of the teacher's skill. Take the advice and use it to grow stronger.

A valuable coach is one that provides a fertile environment for you to grow and evolve into a player of your own. Perhaps Maria Montessori said it best,

> In order to achieve their 'whole self,' a child needs the freedom to achieve through order and self-discipline...Through the use of a 'prepared environment,' the child is encouraged to explore and learn. Self-motivation also plays an important role in the child's learning. The Montessori teacher is there to prepare the environment, direct activities, and offer stimulation to the child. But, it is the child himself who learns; who is motivated through the work itself to persist in his task.

As a general word to coaches, don't underestimate the influence you have on your students or the potential you have to inspire them. Several years ago, I witnessed a perfect example of a coach instilling a self-fulfilling prophecy into one of his players. Player A was a serve and volleyer with a decent, but not great overhead. One day, coach X began boasting to the rest of the team, "Player X may not have terrific volleys, but I'll tell you what, he covers the lob as good as anyone out there." After several days of this, not only did the team start fearing his overhead, but also Player X gained immeasurable confidence in his overhead for the rest of the season. From that point on, he took it as a personal insult if someone tried to lob him. Nothing about his technique changed, but I don't think a lob got over him for the rest of the year. The mark of a good coach is two fold. Not only must he be able to instruct, but he must be able to inspire as well.

> There comes a point in each person's life when he/she asks himself: HOW DO I WANT TO BE REMEMBERED? Reality is so few people have the chance that you have tonight. You have the chance to effect the answer to that question [...] Play with heart. No matter what happens, we don't let up![...] PLAY EVERY SINGLE DOWN LIKE IT'S THE PLAY THAT WILL SAVE THE GAME!
> **—Jim Tressel, OSU Football Head Coach, Fiesta Bowl Pregame Speech, January 4th 2003**

The junior player (and family) – coach relationship can be rocky at times. It is uncommon that an up-and-coming junior player will stick with one coach his entire career for better or worse. Coaches should always realize the reality of the coaching business that the player and the player's family does not *owe* you any loyalty – that is what the dollars are for. As a coach, you must always be prepared for the fact that the player may and probably will leave you at some point. On the other hand, players and their family must always have open lines of communication with the coach and if things are not going well, they must always discuss the situation and try to fix it as amicably as possible.

> *It's just like the relationship that goes south between a woman and a fella – it just doesn't happen in 2 days. Obviously it's been on the woman's mind for a while – she should be telling him all along, 'Hey, you'd better take over the reins or I'm selling stock.'*
> **—Anonymous**

Remember, the best thing the parent of a hard-working kid can do is find a coach who was a good player himself and believes in solid fundamentals. It would truly be a tragedy if a kid willing to work hard and sacrifice is not able to actually use those attributes and spends his entire career searching for the perfect shot. Let your child determine his own fate and not leave it in the hands of some supposed guru. The best players in the nation and on television got there not because they all had a "guru" show them revolutionary techniques and methods, but rather because they had solid guidance and flat out more determination than the rest.

> *There is one true teacher in tennis: try to win every point. It will guide you to be the best player you can be. It will never fail you. The true teacher says, "If it works, keep doing it. If it doesn't, stop immediately." It is the ultimate evolution. Do not become sidetracked in trying to learn what wins and trying to do that. Learn from the true teacher.*

No chapter on coaches would be complete without addressing the "grass is greener on the other side" and "if it ain't broke, don't fix it" factors in making decisions. Many times, an improving player, happy with her current coach, will have an idea planted in her head that another coach can offer her something new and special. Given her ambitious personality, her curiosity and desire to achieve will lead her to switch coaches. Now, this is not necessarily a bad thing, but the player always needs to weigh all the pros and cons. There are two aspects that players usually fail to realize. One, the player should reflect upon her desire to switch coaches – is it truly because the new coach is better, or is it simply her own desire to see what's out there? If she is rationally 50/50, the irrational "grass is greener on the other side" factor can unfortunately sway her decision. Two, the player should not switch unless there is a clear benefit. Oftentimes, when approached with an alternative, players look at it like a fork in the road rather than a detour off of the main route. They do not take into consideration that their current path is successful and that the alternative is a deviation from safety. If the player is rationally 50/50, she should always choose her current path by virtue of its safety, and not flip a coin as if it were a fork in the road. While romantic, the Robert Frost poem, "Two roads diverged in a road, and I – I took the one less traveled by" is not the inspiration on which one should make decisions.

As a word to coaches, do not feel personally slighted if a player leaves you. Oftentimes, you are battling forces beyond your control, forces intrinsic to temptation, and forces enhanced by the Lure of the Big Game.

I gave them a completely convincing argument, but I cannot help it if they choose to act illogically.

Ultimately, ineffective coaches usually have one of the 3 following limitations: he does not have actual playing experience; he did not notice what he experienced; he cannot convey what he experienced to you.

Questions to ask yourself about a coach:

Can the coach explain the deep fundamentals as he has experienced, reflected and developed from his own playing days?
Can the coach give you simplified abbreviations to employ the deep fundamentals, and explain / show you how they stem from the deep fundamentals?
Is the coach simply a collection of pointers and techniques most likely gleaned from other players, coaches or <u>the depths of his own imagination</u>? (Be very wary if the coach shows you examples as "proof" for his ideas, but cannot demonstrate it himself – to be safe, look to take advice from the horse's mouth – i.e., <u>from those who say what they do and do what they say, not from those who say what others do and do what others say</u>)
Is the coach simply passing along to you what he has been taught, yet does not understand and was never able to employ himself?
Does the coach's teachings reach the level of the game itself? Think about chess:
    You can learn how the pieces move and the object of the game
    You can learn opening moves and various effective patterns
    You can learn the guiding principles behind the patterns
    You can learn chess itself
There are many layers of conceptual understanding. Take society for example:
    You have Laws (mechanics / techniques)
    You have Justice (system / intertwined collection of techniques)
    You have Philosophy (reasoning / explanation of system)
    You have The Relationship Between Humans (<u>the</u> very thing you are trying to get at)
While coaches with deep understanding are invaluable, it is better for beginners to have a coach who teaches simple basics rather than one who tries to be too complicated for his own good!

42

Cults

> *Rudeness is the weak man's imitation of strength [...] When the weak want to give an impression of strength, they hint menacing at their capacity for evil. It is by the promise of a sense of power that evil often attracts the weak [...] Our greatest pretenses are built up not to hide the evil and ugly in us, but our emptiness. The hardest thing to hide is something that is not there.*
> **—Eric Hoffer, The True Believer: Thoughts on the Nature of Mass Movement**

In any area of life, there will be cults. As foreign as this concept may seem, you may be closer to one than you suspect. The high emotions, hopes and financial payoffs in tennis are ripe for creating cults. Understand and always be able to recognize the following characteristics of the cult lifestyle.

- Contrary to popular belief, people are not sucked into cults. In their search for the Holy Grail of unbeatable tennis, they dive right in.

- While cults are based on legitimate introductory knowledge, the higher levels of teaching become more and more outrageous. Students at this point, however, are so brainwashed that they are eager to believe anything.

- Cults are centered around a central master who have the defining characteristics:
    - Superior and Exclusive Knowledge which supersedes everyone else's knowledge on tennis.
    - Obscure and Unverifiable Knowledge obtained through a revelation or a distant / unreachable or dead grandmaster.
    - Dismissal of other coaches and Insistence that his way is the only true way to play.
    - Unwillingness to teach beginners in his own school

- Claims credit for good players who train with other coaches.
- Unwillingness or Inability to prove their skill against outside players. Being able to defeat one's own students is not necessarily valid proof of skill. Beware of Self-Promulgated Accolades, where person A builds up person B who in turn builds up person A.
- Uses phrases like "I can fix your game in one lesson" and "Revolutionary."
- Blames the deficiencies in the student if their game does not improve over several years.
- Uses players as "guinea pigs" for new theories which the master dreams up seemingly every week.

• Cults are insular and elitist. Players under this master are attracted to belonging to an elite style of play rather than improving per se.

• Cults have a "we vs. them" attitude which causes conflict in the larger society. Players from other coaches are deemed the enemy and ridiculed.

• Cults place embargos on the players. Almost always to protect revenue or image, players are not allowed train with players of other schools of thought deemed "dangerous" to the cult teaching.

• Association with the Cult undermines familial ties and relationships.

Beware of fallacious logic employed by the Cult. One "truth" commonly used to dupe players is the need to "train for winning in the long run." While this may be true in some instances, it is not an irreducible primary and cannot be used to "prove" everything. Thus, one cannot plan and rationalize all actions based on this rule. These long-term promises of success are not unlike telephone scams conning old grandmothers out of their last savings. People are very susceptible to hearing what they want to hear when things are not going well. Another psychological trap commonly associated with cults is what Ayn Rand calls, Argument from Intimidation. Oftentimes, cultmasters say, "Only a small-minded player with no long-term aspirations would refuse the game of the future – you're not one of them, are you?" The key is to not confuse intellectual evaluation with emotional appeal and approval.

> *We see in our heroes what we want to believe. We build them up in our minds. In that way, they represent our hopes and dreams, and to bring them down, we would be tearing down a piece of ourselves as well. We want them to be the fairy tale that we always sought – but we must also know where the real person ends and where our own ideas begin. Remember, do not make them out to be something they are not just because that is what you*

want. Do not mistake for reality ideas that you project onto things that do not exist.

Cults are born when a group of individuals give up the pride of owning one's own thoughts and devote themselves entirely to professing and dutifully championing the thoughts of another person. While credit always belongs where credit is due, believing that one person's ideas are so perfect that they cannot be improved upon and must be spoken verbatim, and admitting that one's own judgment and insight is so inferior that it warrants selfless submission and blind faith is the type of self-confidence loss and detrimental humility that is ripe for a cult.

The untalented are more at ease in a society that gives them valid alibis for not achieving than in one where opportunities are abundant. In an affluent society, the alienated who clamor for power are largely untalented people who cannot make use of the unprecedented opportunities for self-realization, and cannot escape the confrontation with an ineffectual self.
—Eric Hoffer, The True Believer: Thoughts on the Nature of Mass Movement

Your enthusiasm must always be for the ideas themselves and not transform into a blind enthusiasm for the person who speaks them, for then he is without check. Every idea must stand on its own merit and not on the strength of previous ideas or accomplishments. In the end, you must always be the final purveyor of your own thoughts.

The second time you make a mistake, it's your fault.
Saying sorry means I won't do it again.
Its only a joke if the other guy thinks its funny.
—Ty Tucker

Being skeptical does not mean you are not naïve. Protection against brainwashing arises from having your own core beliefs and opinions, and the self-confidence, egocentricity if you will, that your ideas supersedes those of other people until their ideas are carefully analyzed and explicitly proven superior. The purported or even real authority of the sources should not exempt their ideas from your inner pre-eminence. Skepticism and scrutiny do you no good if you are a tabula rasa with nothing to make judgment. Going into situations with an "I'm right (and you're wrong if you don't agree with me)" attitude is not closed minded, but rather the very least confidence that any self-respecting adult should be afforded. In the same vein, if someone disagrees with you, do not pejoratively label him as stubborn; it is your responsibility to prove your point to them before you can expect them to agree. In the end, remember that scrutiny and skepticism are easily defeated by suggestion, and while unscrupulous individuals always use the open-minded tact to psychologically weaken people before an attack, self-confidence in existing opinions is your best prophylaxis. Indoctrination does not conquer by force. It conquers by Trojan Horse. Having an open mind simply means you are willing to listen, it does not prevent you from passing judgment.

> *When I was in prison, I was wrapped up in all those deep books, that Tolstoy crap – people shouldn't read that stuff.*
> **–Mike Tyson**

If you find yourself associated with a cult-like tennis school or cult-like coach, get out immediately. The fantasy which has been sewn together for you will lead you nowhere towards your dreams. If you are more interested in finding a super shot than building a solid game and fighting for the wins, go buy some video games.

43

Drills

Before you can effectively implement any strategy, you must be able to produce the prerequisite shots. The only way you can develop the solid strokes needed to advance your game is by drilling. Random hitting, although much easier and less tedious, is not sufficient. Keep in mind that behind every great player, is hours upon hours of drilling. There has never been an outstanding player who has not had to go through the process of constant drilling. Perhaps even better proof is in the players who choose not to drill. They are markedly less consistent and have less confidence in even their most basic shots. If you feel that your level of play fluctuates greatly from day to day, or if your game gets abnormally "rusty" within a short time, you are a good candidate for needing more drills.

In music, learning to play a new song is a long and difficult process. Very often, there are a few lines that are especially tricky. While the natural temptation is to keep practicing the entire song, learning the easy parts well and slurring your way through the hard parts, it is much better to repeat the hard parts until you master it. This method may not be as fun, but when recital time arrives, it will ensure that you don't freeze on stage. The same logic applies to tennis. Unless you isolate each stroke and solidify it, you will not have the confidence to use it in a match. Even though you hit a lot of balls by randomly hitting with a partner, this form of practice is very inefficient. Every ball you see is slightly different: some high, some low, some hard, some short. Because you have to constantly improvise your stroke, you cannot form a solid base. This is definitely no way to engender confidence in your game. While there are many drills out there, you must choose the right ones in order to foster good habits. Nevertheless, no matter what drills you use, the most important thing to remember is to always hit with a target in mind.

At first glance, ball machines seems to be the best option for drilling. However, they have several problems. Not only will they hamper your timing, but they cause lazy footwork, mind wandering and other bad habits. While the optimal drilling partner is another player who is willing to help you, hitting against a wall is a better choice than a ball machine.

To develop confidence, solidity and pace in your groundstrokes, have your partner stand at net in either the deuce or ad box and blast groundstrokes at him. Tell him to volley your shots back at a medium speed, depth and height. The objective is not to run you around, but rather to help you get a feel for putaway shots. It is important that you aim for his midsection and not his chest. If he is volleying balls around his shoulders, your shots are headed out. This drill is more effective if you can catch the ball at its peak above the net level and pound it down around his waist. While other drills are designed for consistency, use this drill for developing powerful shots. Try to put a hole through your partner. This is a fun drill, especially for young children!

Once you have mastered the previous drill, you need to practice the infamous side to side baseline drill. However, Carlos Fleming adjusted this drill to make it many times more effective. Using tennis balls, outline the perimeter of a square area of about 5x5 feet in each baseline corner. This type of target is better than a cone or stack of balls because you can judge for each shot whether your ball is landing within the target area. Have your partner stand about 4 feet behind the service line and feed you groundstrokes. However, instead of a simple left right alternating feeding pattern, your partner should mix up the feeds to emulate an actual point and make sure you do not guess the next ball. There are two things you should focus on in this drill. Number one, try to hit every ball into the targets. Even as you tire, do not lose your concentration and throw away your form. Number two, hone your footwork. Make sure you sprint to the ball and then recover by shuffling all the way back to the hash mark. You should not only cut the ball off at a diagonal, but also arrive to your spot before the ball even gets there. This will allow you to align your body, the ball and your target in a straight line. You can tell that you are getting to the ball early enough if you can hold your balance after your stroke and not let your momentum carry you off to the side.

An advance version of this drill actually implements point play. To simulate a point, have your partner feed balls as if he were your opponent. Whenever you miss your target or leave a ball short, he should hit a more difficult feed as if he were attacking you. Your objective should be to set up a point by "drawing" a short ball from your "opponent" with multiple good shots and ending the point at net. To appreciate the value of each point and the impact of unforced errors, keep track of your points. It is important to reinforce the concept of accountability. Start off at 0. For each point fully set up and won, add 1. For every unforced error, subtract 1 (do not be afraid to venture into negative numbers). Keep playing the drill until you reach a set number such as 10. Do not stop with the player "winning" or "losing." Only stop when the set number is accomplished. This prevents the establishment of an easy way out when one gets tired. The incremental advance from drills to point play is the type of stepwise progression players need to improve their game. It requires no leaps of faith or trial and error.

> *This drill will help you appreciate just how difficult it is to defeat an opponent who absorbs all of your free points / unforced errors, does not give any back, and makes you earn every one of your points.*

There are a couple of points to remember during drills. First, aiming for targets is better than simply aiming in a direction. It gives your shots more purpose and increases your accuracy. The best players in the world seem to hit the corners not by any coincidence; they are actually aiming for them. Second, do not pace yourself. If you have 10 minutes of energy left, give 10 minutes of 100% effort and get off the court. Do not give stretch it out to 20 minutes with 50% energy. This suboptimal performance will carry over into matches. Unfortunately, many tennis clinics are conducive for this behavior. Third, the purpose of these drills are not to build up stamina. They are for solidifying your strokes. Your offcourt workouts should condition you to handle the most rigorous of the drills. Fourth, do not use more pace than you can keep the ball in play with. It does no good to practice at 80% pace, but only having confidence to use 50% pace in a match. Instead, practice at 65% pace and once you get comfortable with it, increase all your shots by 1%. When you watch professionals on television, it seems as if they are just rallying, but every shot is very hard because they have built up their confidence to a high percentage of their maximum pace. This phenomenon explains why skinny players who are competent at 85% often outslug stronger players limited to only 50% of their pace.

One of the most useful games you can play is the plain old baseline game where one player feeds the ball in. This format gives you an excellent opportunity to hone your favorite play by numerous repetition. Ideally, you should face many different players so that you can amend your signature combination to handle various styles of play. As with all practice, you should treat each point like you would in a match. Instead of ascribing to the "play like you practice" saying, adopt the "practice like you play" mentality. By always raising your aggressiveness and the pace on your shots in practice to the highest level you are comfortable using in an actual match, you will never succumb to nerves under pressure while still pushing the envelope on improvement. It is important to attend to both drills and point situations during practice.

The baseline game is very important because it represents the "default" position that occurs in tennis and the one in which you absolutely need to have a planned approach to. If given the most common situation of two players at the baseline, and if your opponent takes no specific action (against which you can simply respond), you should have a well practiced set-up and execution of winning the point. Think of it like an offensive player in soccer. Oftentimes, beginners will not have a set way of beating a defender in a one-on-one situation. They will either pass it to a teammate, or "do something" from their "bag of moves" and hope the defender will commit so they can react accordingly. They do not have a signature pattern, or basic *flowchart* of moves they can apply to the defender if he does nothing ("contains" the forward) or makes no mistakes ("does not fall for anything") or plays passively (does not provide anything the forward can "make a move against").

Lining up practice matches is one of the most integral parts of a training regimen. Play with players at your own level and slightly better or worse. Do not avoid rivals in the area; remember it is not he or she whom you are competing with, but rather the larger tennis community. If you are afraid to reveal your game, simply refrain from using your favorite plays. It is useful to find a better player, often older, representative of the highest level of your age / skill bracket. Do not hesitate to pay such a person to occasionally play matches with you – it is well worth it. He can serve as a measure of your progress and a source of confidence in that no one you face in a tournament will be better than him. In all of these practice matches, there is one thing to remember. Always try to win and always put your best weapon forward. If you have to get emotional, then get emotional (just don't be obnoxious).

> Sometimes players get so caught up in trying to learn winning strategies, they begin to see the strategies as the end-goal and think winning will come by itself. This is wrong. Your focused intent must always be winning. The strategies are merely hints to help you win and will not work by themselves – you still have to try to win.

> Most players who have experienced a lot of winning have no problem keeping their eyes on winning, but less successful players are often befuddled by this subtle psychological quandary.

Remember, *you* have to *try* to get what you *want*. When you recognize this *seemingly* basic fact, you will have crossed a major hurdle and will surpass many people. However, without it, you are still in the infancy of competition, and cannot even call yourself ready to win.

44

Before Your Kid Starts Tennis

Appropriately informative, mildly intimidating...
—**Emily Beers**

How early should parents start their child in tennis? There is no definite answer for this question; each child is different in terms of his maturity and readiness for a commitment to the game. If tennis is only a passing recreational activity, there is no criteria for children to play. It is fun and enjoyable. It provides hours of exercise in an outdoor setting.

You can only get good at chess if you love the game.
—**Bobby Fischer**

Research has shown that 75% of all kids drop out of organized sports by the age of 12. The most common reason given is "It just wasn't fun anymore." Going back to the principle of gameness, remember that play, as in child's play, is fun based on the participation of the activity itself. However, as kids mature, their play slowly evolves into competition. In this realm, the actual activity is irrelevant whether it is tennis, gymnastics, or soccer. All that matters is the process itself of discriminating winners from losers. For the hormonal and competitive teenager, there is nothing intrinsically fun about tennis. The only source of fun lies in the act of winning now or the driving hope of winning in the future. Provided that the extent of his success was equal, his satisfaction and level of fun would be the same in any sport. You as an adult may not be able to reconcile this reality in your mind, but remember, you are in a different stage of your life and have already established a fixed understanding of your place amongst your peers.

> *The so-called thrill of competition is better described as the thrill of winning or the thrill of wanting to win. For kids, there is the desire for a nice trophy, a material prize. For teens, there is the desire for a high ranking, an indication of one's reputation and standing amongst peers. In moving from childhood to the teen years, the "hatred for losing" begins to catch up to the "love of winning." As much as one loves what one has won, he or she now feels the need to protect it with as much passion. An effective way to allay this cycle of never-ending anxiety and fleeting exhilaration is to shoot for tangible measures of success.*

> Winning particular tournaments and reaching career milestones are prizes that can never be taken away. If you won the State Tournament in 2004, no one can ever take that away from you. This approach makes competition a much more satisfying experience.

If you are seriously considering competitive tennis designs for your child, be forewarned about the nature of the beast. Just as some types of animals are not starter pets, tennis is not a starter sport. First of all, it takes an exorbitant amount of money to learn tennis fast enough to keep up with other kids. The financial hurdle of entry cannot be overlooked. Even if your child is very gifted, there is no way around lessons, clinics, out-of-town tournaments and egregiously priced equipment. If you have visions of college scholarships dancing in your head, forget it. The reason to enroll your child into tennis lies not in any future financial benefit, but rather in the character gained through competition and training. Indeed, the monetary investment required to reach a college scholarship level of skill far exceeds the price of college. Many parents think they have a child prodigy on their hands. This may be true, but of the hundreds of junior players that are still competitive at a national level in the 18 and under division, each and every one was considered a child prodigy in his own right. To make an outstanding impact, your child will have to be a prodigy amongst prodigies. A higher percentage of baby sea turtles live to breeding age than beginner tennis players that reach a professional level.

Be prepared for tennis to consume all of your child's time. Most likely, it will dominate your life as well. Unlike soccer, football or baseball, tennis is a 12-month a year sport. A month vacation for your child spent getting rusty while his peers are improving may be all that's needed to squander a year's worth of work. At the highest level, it is a rat race, pure and simple. Your child will miss out on many relaxing activities that his friends and schoolmates enjoy. There is no way around the time commitment.

Prepare to become obsessed. Prepare for loss. Prepare for cutthroat competition. Normal relationships may become strained whether your child is winning or losing. Tennis will test your ability as a parent to handle many questions in a field you may know nothing about. Understand that tennis will become ingrained in who your child is. The line between playing tennis and being a tennis player will disappear forever. On the subject of losing your identity, Ralph Waldo Emerson said it best:

> Man is not a farmer, or a professor, or an engineer, but he is all. Man is priest, and scholar, and statesman, and producer, and soldier. In the divided or social state, these functions are parceled out to individuals, each of whom aims to do his stint of the joint work, whilst each other performs his [. . .] Man is thus metamorphosed into a thing, into many things. The planter, who is Man sent out into the field to gather food, is seldom cheered by any idea of the true dignity of his ministry. He sees his bushel and cart, and nothing beyond, and sinks in the farmer, instead of Man on the farm.

Enroll your kid into different activities before tennis. Involvement in other endeavors will form a solid personality and good character based on self-esteem and good parental guidance. When he begins tennis, he will be ready for the competitive stress to try to rip away his even-keeled foundations. Being a well-rounded individual will prevent him from being narrow-minded and getting sucked into a world of its own known as tennis.

> Stephens: *He does nothing but play chess. No other interests.*
> Kingsley: *He goes to school?*
> Stephens: *Oh, no.*
> Kingsley: *Well that's great. You should be proud of yourself.*
> Stephens: *I am.*
> **—Ben Kingsley and Robert Stephens in Searching for Bobby Fischer**

Why should you play tennis? Play tennis for the hope. The hope of greatness in one measure or another. All real tennis players are dreamers. The rigors of the gate will long eliminate those who have lost hope. At a recreational level, tennis is a lifelong sport. At the competitive level, tennis ends with the loss of hope in the dream. Most players give to tennis their life, their time and their dreams. Very few players achieve what they originally set out to do. They must take satisfaction and joy in the many battles fought and the small triumphs along the way. We are forever running uphill, looking forward and chasing the horizon. Perhaps there is no peak, only mountain face. Perhaps this path has no end, existing purely as a globe. Choose your path wisely. It is a long journey.

> *At 19, Ronaldo was the most coveted soccer player in the world. His spectacular goals in the professional league became 10 second highlight reels for thousands of fans...*
>
> *Then things began to crumble. In the 1998 World Cup finals, the much favored Brazilian team faltered against the Zinedine Zidane-led French team. It was one of Ronaldo's worst games, and his reputation took a major hit amongst the 2 billion people who watched.*
>
> *The four following years were injury plagued, and Ronaldo wasn't even the star on his professional team, Inter Milan. Shortly before 2002 World Cup, he started to regain his old form. However, many critics predicted that Ronaldo would fail, once again, to raise his game when it mattered most.*
>
> *But Ronaldo prevailed.*
>
> *In a tournament that featured stars such as England's Beckham, Germany's Klose and Kahn, and Raul of Spain,*

Ronaldo proved himself to be the greatest of them all. He scored 8 goals, 2 in the finals, en route to the title and brought the FIFA trophy back to his native Brazil. He became a national hero and secured his place in soccer lore.

When you play a sport, you strive to become the star you see on TV, the hero of the people. This is where raw determination comes from, where eternal hope lies. No one puts posters on their wall because their dream is to be mediocre. They want to be known as the best – the best on the block, the best in their state, the best in the world, or the best there ever was. When you lose the dream, you lose it all.

We dream of being Jimmy Connors on Stadium Court
We dream of being Don Quixote rising one last time for Dulcinea
We dream of being William Wallace leading the charge against the English

A Man does it for his Glory
A Man does it for his Love
And a Man does it for his People

And as your career draws to a close, even if you realize that being the national championship is not attainable, you will still train for them as if they were, until the very end. That even in your decline, you will not be going downhill, but rather still chasing the horizon, still reaching new hilltops, still improving.

The greatest gift one can have is not raw talent. It is not the ability to work hard. It is the ability to be inspired.

The Vision that you glorify in your mind, the Ideal that you enthrone in your heart – this you build your life by, this you will become.
—**James Allen**

45

Stopping By Woods

Your dream starts like this: you are in a race, and although you started in the back, you find yourself catching up to people and passing them. It seems like you are doing well and you are on your way to the front...and then you pass a field. You notice a little sign that says, "Hidden in this Field is the Secret Sauce: Guaranteed to Make Your Forehand Stupendous." So you think to yourself, "I've got a little lead, I'm doing well – I'll stop here and look for this Secret Sauce. If I can find it, I'll really blow by these chumps." As you are looking around in the field, some people catch up and pass by. You rationalize it to myself, "Oh well, when I get my Stupendous Forehand, it'll be well worth it." Time goes by and you still haven't found the Secret Sauce. Thinking for a moment, you say, "Oh well, I've spend all this time looking for it, I might as well stay until I find it." However, one day, much to your dismay, you realize that you forgot where you put your backhand. It must be lost somewhere in the field! Torn between looking for the Secret Sauce and finding your old backhand, you end up doing a little bit of both. You think to yourself, "As soon as I find my backhand, I'll get back in the race and forget this Secret Sauce." A tiny voice in your head tells you to leave your backhand behind, but you quickly dismiss this thought as you would be nothing without your backhand. You still hold out hope that you can find both your backhand and the Secret Sauce. Time passes and you soon give up all hope of finding the Secret Sauce. You only wish for your backhand back, but it looks like you will turn into an old man looking around in this field. People in the race look at you briefly as they pass by. You see both the pity and disdain in their eyes. Little did they know you were once at the head of the pack. You want so bad to get up, give chase and show them up...but you can't because you are stuck in this field. One day, you summon up your courage. You will get back in the race. You will leave your backhand behind, forever lost in this field. This is the cost of your greed and the price for moving forward again. You give up the hope in a last second miracle of finding your backhand and the Secret Sauce. You have everything you need, and though you are far behind everyone, you will be back in the hunt. Never again will you read small signs on the side of the road and stop to wander in fields. And so, you are back in the race, bloodied but not beaten. The dream continues.

46

Be Your Own Man

Equal to All – Second to None

One cannot stress enough the importance of parental attention during a youngster's childhood. Praise your child and encourage him to succeed. Tennis can serve a pivotal role in your child's development. While teenage culture typically discriminates and ostracizes those with differences, excelling in a particular field can avert this angst. Tell your child not to view a difference as a bad thing, but rather as a unique quality. Many famous celebrities make their signature, yet unusual characteristics attractive. Uma Thurman does not have the stereotypical model face. Notorious BIG is overweight. Remember, if your child can root his self-confidence in his ability in tennis or another sport, the whims and opinions of his peers will not affect him.

> We live not only our lives but, whether we know it or not, also the life of our time. We add to that larger life or detract; we give or withhold, we lead or shrink back, we put ourselves on the line for the truth or we ignore the summons, we meet the great challenge of our age or we retreat to our gardens...to step forward into history, to step into the life of your age, to step onto history's stage and seek to take part constructively, to try to make your era better—that is a very great thing.
> **—Peggy Noonan, Why We Talk About Reagan**

Know that in order to be popular, you must first garner respect from your peers. They have to see that you can stand on your own, that your self-value and happiness is not dependent on other people's approval. As long as they feel they have power over you, they will always treat you with condescension and contempt. You will never be able to stand up for yourself if, in the back of your mind, you still want them to like you. This is the ultimate paradox of popularity and having true friends. You must remember, it is better to attract people with your charisma than to always try to please them. No one wants a fawning friend. At the other end, do not act cool and pretend to be impervious to everything and everyone. Do what *you* find fun. You will meet people who have the same goals.

> When heroes cannot be found, belief that there even are ideals worth living for begins to fade. The standard line

> becomes, "the system stinks," "the system is cruel and unfair," "the people in charge are self-serving hypocrites." And of course, this victim's attitude toward the corrupt and unfair "system" grants him permission not to serve, not to do his required duty, not to try, not to strive for excellence...There was a time in western history when it was believed that every boy wanted, in his deepest self, to be a hero.
>
> That the true hero is not one who seeks ideals, who seeks to be a hero, who feels almost like a martyr striving for excellence, or who is ridiculed by his peers for being a happy slave of conformity. The true hero does what is in his nature, which by virtue of his character, embodies the ideals of a hero.

—Dr. Richard Hawley, University School Headmaster

There is a somewhat common phenomenon amongst unpopular individuals. The unpopular person finds himself without any friends. In an effort to rectify this situation, he tries to get people to like him by accommodating his personality to those of others. However, he soon runs into the fawning friend problem. Next, he tries to "act cool" and be the person everyone wants to be around. This approach has problems as well because others can see through his act. At this point, the unpopular person is at a loss; he can either act cool and have no true friends, or he can be a pushover and be popular in a doormat sort of way. What he needs to do at this point is to remember why he wants friends in the first place. The "no-true-friend / fawning friend" quandary arises when one starts wanting to have friends for the sake of having friends. The unpopular individuals must remember that fun is the basis of making friends. If he approaches others with the mindset that *he* wants to have fun (without being selfish or egocentric), he will not feel pressured to behave a certain way in order to have friends. *He must try to get others to join him in doing what he wants to do for fun.*

What is confidence? It is not needing to hide your desire for something out of fear that you may not get it. Don't be a poser. Some people, however, take this too far. Do not overcompensate and push your differences onto other people in an effort to preempt a potential attack. Stay the middle course. Your strengths will protect you and give you pride. Your weaknesses will keep you humble and teach you to trust. Together, they will allow you to open your heart to others and live life with love.

> A man's depth is not measured by how eloquently he can speak about philosophy, but rather by the depth of his values, the level on which he connects with others, and the genuineness of his soul.

47

Tennis as a Teacher

> *True confidence is not about knowing you can do something if you really wanted, but rather the willingness to really want something.*

Tennis will undoubtedly help you understand and see through the many pitfalls hidden within society. Instead of being a society follower, you will be a society leader, paving the way and ushering in new ideals. The questing man is always in a state of becoming while the static man is more interested in his state of being. You will learn the value of sacrifice and investment, and the discipline to resist temptation. If nothing else, these essential virtues are the greatest gifts that tennis offers.

The inherent value of sports lies in its unsophistication and unavoidable tendency to purge the human soul of the falsities presented to us in society. It is easy to lose sight of what really is important in life when surrounded and bombarded by the agenda of today. Christopher Lasch writes on the "Theater of Everyday Life":

> *In ordinary men and women, an escalating cycle of self-consciousness—a sense of the self as a performer under the constant scrutiny of friends and strangers. Reality thus presents itself [. . .] as an impenetrable network of social relations—as role playing, the presentation of the self in everyday life. To the performing self, the only reality is the identity he can construct out of the materials furnished by advertising and mass cultures, themes of popular film and fiction, fragments torn from a vast range of cultural traditions [...] Our selfhood [has come] to depend on the validation of others.*

Tennis provides a welcome respite from the pressures of pop culture and creates an arena for each player to discover his true self. The isolation achieved within your mind and the walls of the court defines a self awareness and inner confidence independent of others. Without an outlet, you risk disappearing as a person and existing simply as the image you see in the mirror. Many people today "confuse successful completion of the task at hand with the impression [they] make or hope to make on others." Even the appearance of spontaneity and actions countercurrent to cultural homogeneity may, in its own right, be only a ploy to achieve a new kind of societal role. Even the workplace is not safe. Lasch writes, "In our times, the elimination of skills not only from manual work, but from white collar jobs as well has created conditions in which labor power takes the form of personality rather than strength or intelligence." With the 21st century rolling on, we must preserve tennis and sports as a whole and prevent it from becoming adulterated by pop culture and "the menace of conformity." As sports as a whole become more sensationalized "for the audience's entertainment" and falls victim to society's encroaching showmanship, it will lose its appeal as a true distinguishing test of excellence and will reduce players into actors. If true sport dies at the hands of our shame of genuineness, the line between how to act and how to live will be lost.

> *In a society that is Just – permitting one to seek happiness as long as it does not infringe upon another – sports and capitalism are the two arenas in which it is acceptable to be selfish at the expense of others. Rules of competition exist, but the glory of unbridled desire is what makes sports a necessary outlet from the society. We must be Just in society, but fierce in sports*

Today's society is being overwhelmed by an addiction to instant gratification. With no end in sight, this alarming trend may lead to an eventual collapse of our cultural structure. Like Aesop's fable of the industrious ants and the indifferent grasshopper, we are headed towards lean winters. Tennis mirrors life and prepares you to handle the hardships of the real world. It is a long journey and you will see many players who do not have the mind or guts to pass the rigors of the game and who eventually quit. If you reach the finish line still on your feet, you will be ready to face almost any obstacle or temptation thrown your way. Truly, to succeed in tennis, you must believe in tomorrow and be willing to work for it with no guarantees.

> *Intelligence is not measured by how many facts one knows or how well one can quote famous thinkers. The truly intelligent person has creativity, originality, and the ability to synthesize that which he has into something better.*

As a last word of advice, know that tennis and all similar endeavors in life are fun only when you have something you can fall back on. For a teenager, being able to pursue tennis on top of being a good student is like having a free shot to see how good you can be at something. It is a chance to dream for something bigger, but remember, having good grades underneath you is what separates you from the stargazers.

> *I entered the Tunnel of Tennis as a young teenager. All this time, I always saw myself as how I was when I entered. However, now that I have emerged, I find it strange how much I have aged since it all began.*

48

At the End of the Day

Rise my friend. Do not take stock in being normal. You are a leader, a hero. We look up to you for you are the last of the good guys, the last bastion of character. Press onward where we could not. Do not let us bring you down, do not let us tell you that mediocrity is better. Do not compromise yourself to conform to the transient trends of society. Don't stop, don't ever stop. There is no glory in the ordinary, only the extraordinary. This is your life, your only chance to be someone. Many years from now, you never want to look back and say, I could have been so good. Woulda, Coulda, Shoulda. You want to look back with satisfaction and be able to tell yourself at the bottom of your heart that you could not have done any better. Are you doing everything right now to be the best you can be? Your body is strong, but not for long. Is your mind willing? You have one chance, one existence, one youth. No regrets. What are you waiting for? C'mon!

> *To dream the impossible dream,*
> *To fight the unbeatable foe,*
> *To bear with unbearable sorrow,*
> *To run where the brave dare not go.*
>
> *To right the unrightable wrong,*
> *To love pure and chaste from afar,*
> *To try when your arms are too weary,*
> *To reach the unreachable star.*
>
> *This is my quest,*
> *To follow that star --*
> *No matter how hopeless,*
> *No matter how far.*
>
> *To be willing to give*
> *when there's no more to give*
> *To be willing to die*
> *so that honor and justice may live*
>
> *To fight for the right*
> *Without question or pause,*
> *To be willing to march*

Into hell for a heavenly cause.

*And I know if I'll only be true
To this glorious quest
That my heart will be peaceful and calm
when I'm laid to my rest.*

*And the world will be better for this,
that one man scorned and covered with scars
still strove with his last ounce of courage.
To reach the unreachable star.*

—Lyrics from <u>Man of La Mancha</u>

Beautiful writing is not in the words – it is in the message. In their purest form, words are but an invisible medium through which the reader can behold the message exactly as it is. Words are not meant to hide or exaggerate, but rather to serve as the mind connection between the writer and the reader. One cannot simply be a writer – one must be a liver of life, first and foremost.

49

Averting Tennis Injuries: Cramps

Tennis is a demanding sport, and there are several common injuries players often run into. Some can be prevented with prophylactic measures, but most people wait until they occur before finding a solution. Although this list does not cover every possible thing that could go wrong, it includes the most practical and effective measures to combat many widely encountered problems.

The number one most misunderstood phenomenon is cramps. On a hot day, players will predictably suffer from dehydration and then cramp up and default. This can all be prevented very simply. First, look in your local grocer for salted pretzels. Ideally, they should have at least 500mg of sodium per serving. Eat 5 or 6 servings the night before your match. The salt will help your body absorb as much water as possible. In order to work, your kidneys need salt to prevent all your water from being urinated out. When your urine is clear, it does not necessarily mean you are hydrated. You are simply urinating out all the excess water your body cannot absorb. However, if your body does not have any salt, it cannot absorb any water and may still have an ion imbalance.

Optimally, the night before your match, you should drink a few glasses of water until your urine is a light yellow. Then you should eat salted pretzels (pretzels are a tasty and effective way to absorb a high amount of salt) and drink about ¾ gallon of water until your urine is clear (credit: Phil Metz). On match day, you do not have to continue drinking more water than you normally would. An hour before your match, your urine should not be completely clear. If it is, it means that your body is still carrying around water it cannot use. This water is dead weight and causes annoying bathroom breaks.

> Ty: *So how does C.J. play?*
> Jeremy Wurtzman: *I heard he got cramps and almost died on the court.*
> Ty: *Well, I don't think we can count on him dying tomorrow*

The main reason behind cramps is not so much a lack of water in your system, but rather a lack of salt to allow your body to absorb the water you do drink. During exercise, your body exudes salt through your pores. On a hot day, you can sometimes see and taste the salt on your skin left behind when your sweat evaporates. If you hydrate and salt properly before a match, it would take a force of nature to give you cramps. In the slim case it should occur, the most common treatments of drinking water, stretching and rubbing your muscles will not help get rid of the cramps. These may temporarily relieve them, but will not prevent them from coming back in 3-5 minutes.

Cramps are caused when your muscles contract and cannot relax. In physiology, the phenomenon that explains this is that your muscle fibers need salt ions to reverse the contraction reflex. The only way to cure cramps is to get those cells sufficient sodium and potassium ions. Short of getting intravenous fluid, salted pretzels are the way to go. As soon as you feel an impending bout of cramps, start eating pretzels. This will alleviate the cramps once the salt and some accompanying water gets into your system. On a nearly empty stomach, this will happen very fast, probably in the span of 2 games or 5 minutes, a short enough time span to salvage your match. On a side note, there can be one other cause of muscle cramps. If you are in poor cardiovascular shape and cannot deliver enough oxygen to your muscles, your muscle cells will accumulate too much lactic acid from anaerobic conversion of pyruvate to lactate. This however, is far less common than dehydration.

Now, the question about sports drinks. They will neither fully prepare you for an intense battle nor will they cure cramps nearly fast enough for you to win your match once cramps are in session. The sports drinks with the highest amounts of sodium and potassium (electrolytes) have only about 160mg per serving. To get the same burst of salt you can get from eating 500 mg of pretzels, you would need to drink much more, probably getting you bogged down and unable to run as well. I do not advocate drinking sports drinks during the match as well. If you hydrate and salt the night before, you will have no need for the small amount of salt they provide. On a hot day, you will end up drinking more of the sweet tasting sports drink and not enough water.

Some people advocate sports drinks because of the sugar and energy calories they provide. However, if you ate and digested a proper prematch meal of carbohydrates like pasta and bagels, you should have plenty of energy stored up. In addition, sports drinks erode your mental toughness. As you get tired, you will begin to desire a taste of your cold drink on the sideline and subconsciously you want to get there, not giving your all to battle out the tough points. It will weaken your resolve to win and redirect your focus on getting to the changeover. Even if this does not seem likely, it happens. Do not give yourself the option of bailing out. As good as the refreshing ice cold sports drink tastes after a long point, it will not taste half as good as coming out of a tough battle with a win.

Although the type of water you drink may seem inconsequential, do not let such a preventable factor hinder your performance. While tap water is regulated by the EPA and rarely causes any problems, it is always smart to have a supply of bottled water for hydration. Many tennis tournaments are played in unlikely places, and no one wants to drink rust colored or funny tasting water. When you go to the grocery store, you will be faced with an array of choices. Always opt for drinking, purified or distilled water over spring water.

The problem with spring water is that its exact content is not constant. While the first three types of water are all purified through ionization, distillation or reverse osmosis, the FDA mandates that spring water cannot be processed to change its basic mineral content. Even if you like the taste of one brand of spring water, every bottling company finds its water in different underground aquifers. Very often, your stomach will be irritated by spring water, leading you to drink less and feel slightly nauseated. When given the option, do not take a chance with spring water, especially if you intend to drink it during your match.

50

Averting Tennis Injuries: Ankles, Shins and Behind Your Knee

As a general rule, most tennis-related pain, other than acute trauma, is the result of insufficient muscle around the area. Although the rest and ice method may help and is the typical knee-jerk response to injury, you need to focus on strengthening the problematic area. Because it is often difficult to find an exercise that pinpoints the right muscles, the following sections cover several of the more common ailments usually not well addressed by conventional physical therapy.

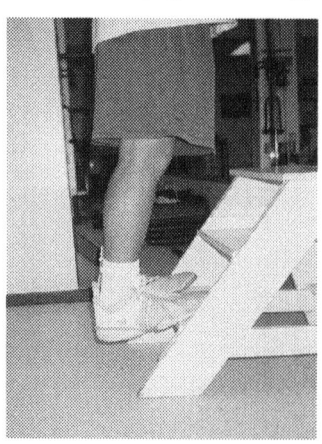 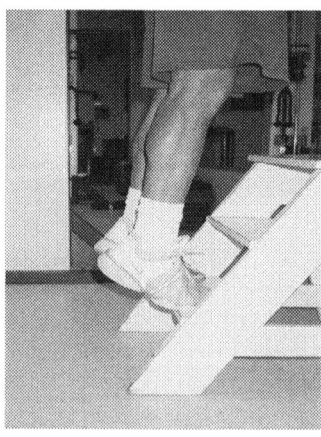

Many players suffer from weak ankles, sore shins and a pain behind the knee area. While icing and rest may temporarily alleviate the pain, these treatments are merely delaying their recurrence and not curing the problem. In tennis, your calf muscles play a largely underestimated role in tennis movement. The above ailments can be prevented by having strong calves to solidify and stabilize your knee and ankle areas that endure pounding day after day. Being able to plant your foot with confidence that it will support your body weight and being able to stop and change directions lie in the strength of your lower legs. You do not want to have to take several stopping steps to halt your body momentum in one direction. You do not want the threat of rolling an ankle in the back of your mind.

The best exercise for your calves is calf raises. Stand at the edge of a stair with the back half of your foot hanging over the edge. Now, raise and lower yourself at least 150 times until you feel a distinct tightening in your calves (gastrocnemius and soleus muscles). Your up and down motion should be slow but continuous, stopping neither at the peak nor the bottom. If you feel the tightening more in your Achilles' tendon area or in the muscles inferior to the head of your gastrocnemius, you are too far off the stair and are using your toes to hang onto the edge. Do not hold weights or use a weight machine for your calves because it is difficult to isolate the proper muscles.

51

Averting Tennis Injuries: Elbow and Wrist

Another part of the body that is subject to many pains is the elbow and wrist. If you have pain on the outside of the elbow (tennis elbow), you need to worry less about fixing your arm and more about fixing your horrendous backhand form. For all the other ailments, there are two exercises that are invaluable in preventing and curing the problem.

 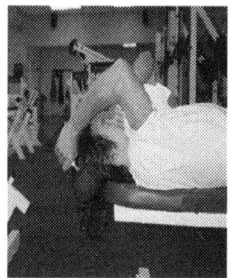 

Use an EZ curl bar to do bicep curls. Your hands should be positioned on the slanted portion of the bar (see picture). Put enough weight onto the bar to feel your forearm muscles getting a workout. With your wrists flexed inward as you curl the bar, you should feel the muscles attached to your medial epicondyle (that knob on the inside of your elbow) tighten up. Do as many reps as possible.

To cure the pain behind your elbow, take a dumbbell and lie down on a bench. You will have to experiment with the amount of weight that is appropriate for you. Raise your arm with the dumbbell so that your upper arm is perpendicular to the ground (see picture). Now, let your elbow bend to about a 45-degree angle and straighten it out again using your triceps. Moving in a slow and controlled motion, you should feel the area that connects your elbow and triceps getting a workout. If you cannot, let your elbow bend more acutely until you do feel it. Use enough weight, and do enough reps until you can feel a distinct tightening in those muscles.

52

Averting Tennis Injuries: The Midsection

 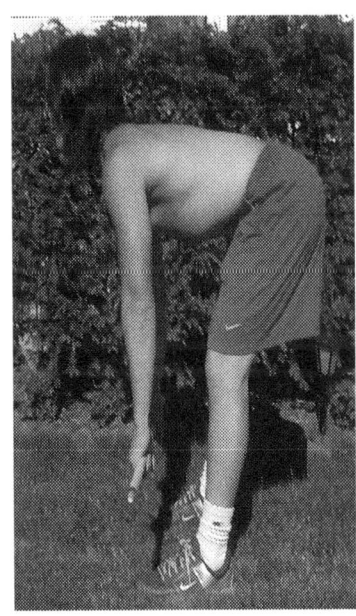

One of the most important yet neglected areas in a tennis player's body is the midsection. A common complaint is lower back pain. Together with a strong stomach, a strong lower back will not only prevent torso injuries, but also help with balance and endurance. During a workout, I advocate doing back exercises before addressing the stomach. The most helpful back exercise is the barbell straight-back stiff-legged deadlift. Holding a weighted bar with both hands, keep your legs and hands shoulder width apart (unweighted stick used in picture). With your chest out and lower back in good posture and not slumped over, bend at the waist slowly and then straighten up again. Have a slight knee bend to protect your lower back. Use enough weight so that after 10 reps you feel some tightness in your lower back muscles. However, never sacrifice good posture for more weight. Because this exercise is so effective in strengthening, you do not need to do it more than two or three times a week. Straight leg bendovers are excellent for strengthening the hamstrings as well.

Although there are numerous exercises to give your stomach a workout, there are three that are most efficient in developing the upper, lower and sides of your midsection. Lie on your side with your legs bent at the knees and hips. You should be in a semi-relaxed fetal position. Simultaneously lift your legs and upper body off the ground as high as you

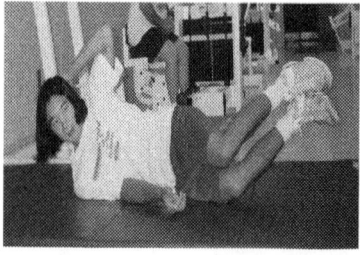 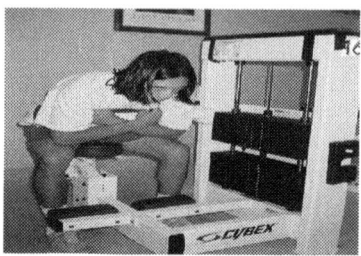

can (see picture). Raise and lower yourself in a controlled rhythm. You should feel the sides of your abs getting a workout.

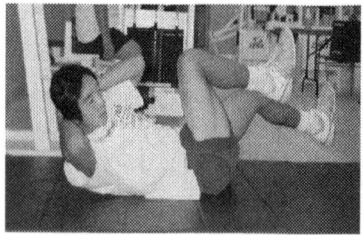 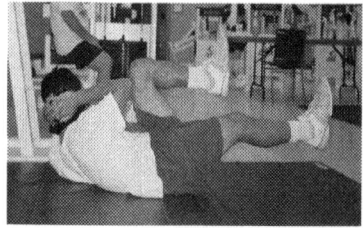

Now, lie on your back. Simulating riding a bicycle with your legs and keeping your hands behind your head, bring your elbow to touch your opposite knee in a twisting motion as you pedal your imaginary bike (see pictures). There is no need to hold the position at any point, but rather keep moving in a medium and continuous speed. The bicycle crunch trains your upper abs.

For your lower abs, you need an ab crunch machine (see picture). The best kinds have an arm on which you can add weight and push down on. On some models, it is very important to wear your seatbelt to keep you in the seat. Notice how my arms are crossed over the bar. Alternate which arm is on top or else the strength of your left and right side abdominal muscles will become uneven. Ideally, you want to add as much weight as you can keep down. You can use your body weight to push the bar down from its initial position. If you feel your back is at all strained, reduce your range of motion and do not go all the way up. It is not necessary to let the arm return to its original position for each crunch. Remember, if you want abs that show, there are two aspects: the muscles have to be big enough (i.e., use high weight exercises), and there cannot be too much fat covering it up (i.e., do cardio to burn it off).

53

Miscellaneous Pearls

For many players who train primarily on hardcourts, learning to play on clay can be a daunting task. The most difficult pitfall to avoid is probably groin pulls. Before you step onto a clay court, you must pay extra attention to strengthening your groin muscles. To do this, you need to use a hip adduction weight machine found in most fitness clubs (see picture).

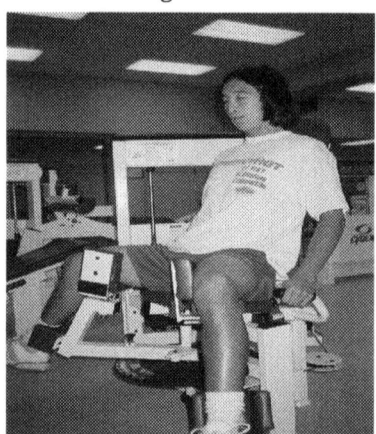 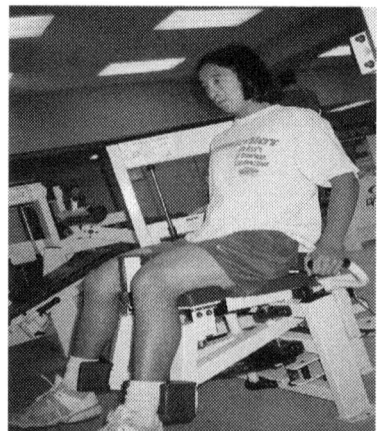

Whether it is the upright model or the seated model, you need to tighten your groin muscles to prepare for sliding on clay.

Remember, no matter how much you lift, only cardiovascular exercise and a low-fat diet will help you become ripped. Try preparing your own food such as steamed rice, plain pasta and trimmed meat. Restaurants can hide oil and fat in even seemingly innocuous foods. Rice-filled burritos, pre-buttered bread and fatty meats are several culprits often incognito. Slowly weaning yourself off of these less healthy choices will do wonders for your game.

There are two ointments that deserve note concerning tennis. Sunscreen can be your friend, or it can cause more problems than your opponent. To prevent it from running into your eyes, apply the sunscreen early enough so that it can absorb into your skin before you start sweating. This, however, will not keep it from making your grip slippery. After rubbing on your sunscreen, wash your hands with soap and water.

Because of the chemical composition of sunscreen, simple water will not do the trick. Soap has polarized particles that bind to the sunscreen droplets and whisk them away.

(green container)

Tennis players who put in many hours of practice are rewarded with calloused, chapped and cracked-skin hands. Ordinary hand creams and lotions are not powerful enough to heal your skin fast enough. The most useful ointment to cure dry skin is Bag Balm, available at many fine drugstores. Apply this at night and cover the affected area with bandages. You will notice a drastic improvement in the condition of your skin.

Oftentimes, after a hard abdominal and back workout, you will feel that you need to crack your back, but can't seem to twist it in exactly the right way. Try this maneuver for creaks refractory to other measures. It yields results as effective as getting it cracked by a professional orthopedist.

Get a flat bench about 2 feet off of the ground (similar to the ones used for bench press). Lay down perpendicular to the bench with the middle of your back across the bench and your feet on the ground (your lower back should be suspended between the bench and your legs (see picture). Now, flex your stomach muscles as if you are going to do crunches from this position. Keep them flexed, but slowly allow your upper body to descend over the bench as if you are going to do a backbridge over the bench. You should feel your back crack very satisfactorily as you let your back descend.

Remember, for those of you who want to develop big muscles, you are going to have to put on a little fat. It is very difficult to stay ripped and get significantly bigger. Your muscles need energy to maintain their size. If, in the course of the day, you become slightly hypoglycemic (low fuel), your body begins breaking down its reserves. First, it looks to fat cells, but if you don't have any, it will begin breaking down your muscle protein. This is why professional body builders need to follow such an exact diet schedule. They need to walk the fine balance of providing just enough food to maintain body energy levels, but not too much that the body begins storing it as fat. Hence, unless you are going to adhere to a strict regimen of caloric intake, it is easiest to put on a thin layer of fat to hold you over during periods of relative fasting.

Another pearl for those who want to develop muscle mass is to eat protein as soon as possible after your workout (within 10 minutes). Your body responds to the stress very quickly and needs those amino acids to rebuild.

During a tournament, if you get a bloody nose, the best way to stop it not the traditional ice pack, steady pressure, or backward head tilt. What you need to do is to keep your head level and raise the arm on the same side as the bleeding nostril straight up in the air. It is strange, but true! (The mechanism may lie in your body redirecting bloodflow from arteries running to your head into arteries running into you raised arm) At any rate, it is a good fact to remember because you wouldn't want to be penalized, or worse yet, defaulted because you couldn't stop a bloody nose during an injury time out (the normal time it takes for blood to clot in a unchecked bleed can be over 5 minutes, especially with elevated blood pressure, as in during exercise).

There is a common belief in tennis that getting too muscular can be detrimental to your game. However, this is only if you cannot move the added bulk. With the stationary bike regimen described previously, this should no problem whatsoever. Taking that into consideration, here are several "high yield" exercises for building strength, mass and definition:

1. Concentration and Preacher Bicep Curls (use supinated grip and hammer grip to work on different bicep muscle groups)
2. Lat Pulldowns
    a. Palms Facing Away (wide grip) – behind the neck
    b. Palms Facing You (shoulder width grip) – in front of neck
3. One Arm, Reverse Grip Tricep Pressdowns
4. Dumbbell Tricep Kickbacks
5. Dips
6. Military Shoulder Press
7. Dumbbell Bent Over Rows
8. Bench Press (see http://users.rcn.com/dl.interport/bench.html) – MM2K "Add 50 lbs to Your Bench Press" Program
9. "Straight-Arm Pec Circles" (see diagram)

Three Points:

- Instead of lifting as much weight as possible, as many times as possible every workout, develop an alternating routine. To increase your max on any muscle group, lift medium weight with high reps one day, then lift high weight with low reps a few days later. This provides better stimulus to your muscles for maximal improvement.

- There are about 3500 calories per pound of fat – however, one cannot say that burning 3500 calories of fat during exercise will help you lose one pound of fat. Your body has many hormones that will affect this figure (mostly to prevent weight loss). A better way to look at cardio exercise is as raising your basal metabolic rate. Short bursts of high intensity exercise is more conducive to this than long sessions of low intensity exercise. The calories you burn *during* short high intensity exercise may be less, but it is more effective at raising your basal metabolic rate and allows you to burn more total calories during the *entire day*.

- Oftentimes, athletes develop a set routine of their favorite exercises and never deviate from it. This leads to a gradual plateau of improvement. Exercises that were high-yield initially will lose their effectiveness as your body gets used to it. The key to constant improvement is varying your workout and stressing your muscles with new exercises. An exercise that seemed ineffective or uncomfortable at first may become your favorite as your body and workout routine matures.

Above sequence: "Straight-Arm Pec Circles" – keep arms straight throughout range of movement.

Upper Back Exercise

Shoulder Raises:
Use various handholds to vary muscle group – thumb down, palm down, thumb up.

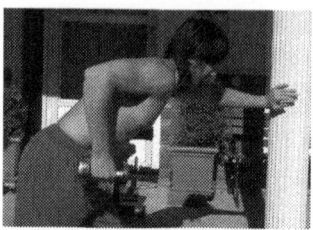

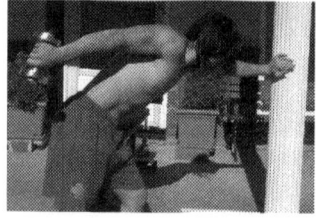

Position for Back Stretch

Tricep Kickbacks

54

Speed and Stamina

There is no single attribute that can win you more matches than speed and stamina. These following exercises are all you need to have explosiveness and endurance. This regimen will give even the most uncoordinated and athletically ungifted players amazing court coverage.

 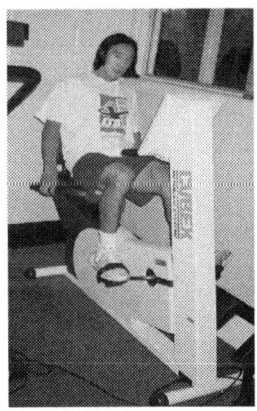 

The first step in improving your movement and conditioning is getting on an electric reclined stationary bike. Increase the pedal resistance in 'manual' mode until you feel like you are pedaling through sand. The most important thing to remember is that you are training your thighs first, then your heart and breathing. If you do not feel your quads really straining to move the pedals, the resistance is not high enough. Pedal as hard as you can for 90 seconds and then rest for 90 seconds. Repeat this cycle at least 4 times. Your target rpm (rotations per minute) range should be at least 75-90 rpm. While you bike, you are also training your heart and lungs. After biking, your thighs should feel tight and your heart should be racing. If either of these are not happening, you did not set the pedal resistance high enough. To further build your conditioning, lower your rest period and increase your sets. Remember it is better to do a little everyday than to burn yourself out doing a lot once in a while. You will find an amazing increase in explosiveness, the ability to start and stop on a dime, and lasting power. While the stationary bike builds endurance and strength, you should use agility drills to build footspeed and develop natural movement on the court. As with all of these exercises, check with your doctor before attempting them and stop if you feel dizzy or lightheaded at any point.

Many players prefer to do leg press or squats instead of biking. These are inferior exercises because in tennis, you need to be able to explode powerfully many times and not to just push a huge amount of weight a few times. Other players do bike, but set the resistance fairly low. The reason for setting the bike at high resistance is that Work = Force x Distance and Power = Work / Time = Force x Distance / Time = Force x Speed. In order to generate more power, you can increase either the speed or the force. Pedaling even 1.5 times faster is nearly possible, but increasing the force of each rotation many fold while maintaining speed increases power quickly..

The spider drill is designed to train your ability to track down balls (see diagram). Starting at the hash mark, sprint and touch each intersection of lines on the court with your foot (not your hand). There are 8 destinations in the following order: the 2 doubles sidelines on the baseline, the T, the 2 sidelines at the service line, the 3 places where the service box touches the net. After touching each spot, back pedal and touch the hash mark with your foot. For the two spots on the baseline sidelines, do not backpedal, simply turn and sprint back to the hashmark. Do not shuffle or sidestep.

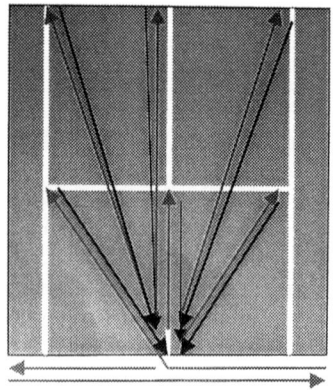

There are a number of pointers to focus on. Number one, time yourself. The idea is to finish the drill as fast as you can. Do not start the drill until you feel fresh. Your movement should be clean and snappy, not sloppy or sluggish. Number two, try to be as explosive as possible. Start facing the net, drop to base stance and explode to the sideline. Beginning in a runner's stance is impractical for tennis. Instead of having your timer say "go," have him start the clock when you make your first move. This will let you work on your first move. Explode like the Roadrunner from the Warner Brothers cartoon: "vanish in the blink of an eye!"   Number three, to further decrease your time, make your turns as efficient as possible. Do not run to the sideline, plant your foot and then change directions. Redirecting your momentum like this wastes precious split seconds. You should not have to stop your momentum and then start it again in the next direction with the same foot. As you are about to touch the line with your foot, you should already be turning your body around before you pivot. As your foot comes down on the line, you should already be facing the opposite direction, ready to sprint forward. When I was learning this drill, I envisioned stopping on a tennis court similar to a hockey stop on ice. It is the most efficient way to change directions. If you do not understand this concept, just do the drill and try to keep making it faster. Your body will naturally discover the quickest way to move. At a certain point, you will realize that the only way to improve your time is by sharpening your starts and turns. This is analogous to tennis movement.

The sidestepping drill is designed to train your recovery movement. Shuffle back and forth between one singles sideline and the hashmark. At each side, touch the lines in a squatting movement without hunching over with your back. Bend with your knees and have both palms touch the ground. Do this drill in 30-second intervals with 30 seconds rest in between. Instead of working on outright speed, concentrate on disciplined movement at a quick but not all-out pace. There are several points to focus on. One, never pop up or stand up straight. Pretend that there is a low ceiling that you cannot hit with your head. Two, your upper body should be still while your legs move. Your arms should be poised and not used to propel yourself. Three, your feet should not touch each other at any time during the movement. Do not gallop and avoid tapping your feet against each other when they come to the middle.

During an actual point, you should explode with a quick first step and sprint to the ball. After hitting the ball, you should have a strong pushback step followed by shuffling recovery. Even if you have a lot of distance to cover to get back to the middle, you should never cross your legs or take large leaps. Moving in a disciplined fashion will allow you to stop and change directions if your opponent tries to wrong foot you.

Keep in mind that your lateral movement is slightly dependent on your leg curvature and bone structure. Bowlegged people tend to have better lateral movement, more developed quadriceps muscles and concomitantly are at less risk for ACL / anterior cruciate ligament tears. On the other hand, people with straight legs or slight knock-knees have better jumping ability perhaps due to more vertical alignment of the upper and lower leg bones.

The jump rope is a valuable training tool. However, most players are not intense enough with it. Instead of doing thousands of skips for hours on end, do double jumps (two rope revolutions for each jump). Although it takes a bit more athleticism, the cardiovascular and dynamic muscular benefit is much greater. Try doing multiple short sets with rest in between. Work your way towards a goal – 100, 300 double jumps in a row.

To train for tennis properly, you must address each aspect of speed. The stationary bike will build up your cardiovascular strength and train your body to feed your muscles the oxygen they need. Weight lifting builds up the size of your muscular fibers. The above described agility drills are designed to condition your fast twitch muscles for quick movement.

55

A Winning Formula

1) <u>Never fall for the Lure of the Big Game</u>: Use Winning as your guide
2) Recognizing and Repeating Success → Improvement. <u>Continual and Active Experimentation does not lead to Improvement</u>. Perfect what you have. Improvement will come by trying to win against better competition.
3) Physical Preparation
   a) <u>Stationary Bike</u>
   b) Spider Agility Drill
   c) Salt and Water
4) Strategical Preparation
   a) Have a system
   b) No free points (unforced errors)
   c) Focus and capitalize in terms of holds and breaks
5) Junior Development
   a) Research to find a good player for a coach
   b) Consistency wins matches
   c) Juniors must always feel that the dream is pursued under their own initiative and that they are not training because their parents instructed / advised them to.

In the end, the key to succeeding in tennis is rather simple. First, get a few free points with your first serve. Second, play solid tennis off the baseline (i.e., no free points, no short balls, and no compromising patterns). Third, use one weapon to put pressure on your opponent when he leaves balls short or starts to push. Fourth, be in good shape and establish the right mindset. Fifth, play a lot of matches and gain experience. Sixth, don't fall for any of the common pitfalls along the way.

THE PLAYER'S CREED:
1. *I DON'T BEAT MYSELF* (unforced or mental errors, bad patterns)
2. *I AM TOUGH TO BEAT* (fast, fighting spirit, tenacious defense, no weaknesses)
3. *I PUNISH MY OPPONENT IF GIVEN AN OPPORTUNITY* (high percentage offense, using patterns to set up my strengths)

Final Words

Tennis is truly more than a sport. It has taught me about people, life and myself. Let me end by reading to you what tennis has meant to me and how it has prepared me for future endeavors.

In high school, my best friend once gave me very valuable advice. He said, "We can neither choose nor know our destiny, all we can do is to try to head in the right direction each day and trust that it will eventually take us where we ultimately want to go." Over the past four years in college, I have come to realize the profundity of his statement. In every aspect of life, we must always look forward, valuing today more than yesterday and working today for tomorrow. It is a lifestyle that is both rewarding and demanding.

Since childhood, I have always set my sights on becoming a physician. Plato once wrote, "In a truly Just state, the soldiers are the most courageous and virtuous, the rulers are the most selfless and wise." Likewise, doctors must be ambitious and persistent, yet dependable, humble and temperate. There is no greater opportunity to make an impact in the world both for oneself and for others. It is my heartfelt belief that true happiness, when the veils of passion and ego are removed, is revealed as a oneness with all life and humanity existing in the same blue ocean of reality. To discover the connection between you and your fellow human mirrors the doctor-patient relationship. Becoming a physician is making a promise to always be a protector and caretaker of the fragile, yet beautiful sanctity of life.

Dedication to see things through to the end has brought me success not only on the court, but in the classroom as well. The standards I try to set for myself in academics are not goals, but rather minimums, below which I cannot accept. In the medical field, where patients straddle life and death, I do not believe falling short is an option. However, after playing hundreds of tennis matches for over a decade, I have realized that there comes a time when even the most Herculean effort cannot guarantee success. Nevertheless, college athletics and team tennis has taught me that in the most difficult trials and tribulations, we carry the burden of not only our fate, but also the hope and dreams of those who rely, depend and look up to us.

The future is never clear; we can only try to head in the right direction. As in tennis, I will prepare myself for tomorrow so that although I may lose some battles, I will never have to rue a lost opportunity.

Good Luck!

Grant me the Humility that I am not better than anyone and the Pride to accept only the best from life.

Thank You:

Mom and Dad, for always listening with love,
          offering sound advice,
          being there to see my accomplishments,
          looking out for me,
          believing in me,
          encouraging me,
          reading me stories,
          being proud of me,
          and always being there for me,
          Mommy and Daddy.

Olivia, for running alongside me until I was steady. You can do it, C'mon!

Grandma, for 5 virtues blossoming: Virtuousness, Wisdom, Sportsmanship, Sociability, and Artistry.

伍育興

Acknowledgments:

Ty, for believing that "The crème rises to the top...and the crud sinks *right* to the bottom." "I feel your pain." Special thanks for always making practice inspiring and always wanting to win.

Carlos, for the discipline to stand up straight and always run through the finish line.

Becky, for teaching me patience and care.

Mark, for being the best friend anyone could ask for.

Phil, for reminding me that "Tennis is not a funny game, it's just played by funny people."

Ryan, for always providing a unique brand of entertaining and more often than not, sardonic humor.

Peter Lau, for having the foresight that I'd need a backhand down the road.

Doug Bloom, for "knowing the level out there."

The Buckeyes, for always fighting to the bitter end.

Dr. Raman, for being an inspiration and an exemplar physician.

Dr. O'Neil, Dr. Hawley, Mrs. Mason, Mrs. Minnillo, and all the teachers at U.S. for teaching me the power of creative and critical thinking.

Manuela
Jason S., Rob G., Scott and Jeff M., Isaac and Tug
Marc, John and Kelvin; Yun-Sheng, Wendy and Joy
The BBHHS Bees – David vs. Goliath (N.O.S.O.) – Wadsworth 1990
Paul W, for endless baseline games and having the most creative buzz ever

Uncle Danny and Aunt Cathy, Grandpa, Aunt Joyce and Aunt Macy, Uncle Charles, David, Alan, Nelly, Ruthie, Debby, Tom Dimofski, Mark Wurtzman, Ben, Brooke, Rocco, Coach Ray, Oden Ray, Joe Raduka, Mrs. Rita, Mr. Jones, Cha-Cha and last but not least, Vinny's Pizza and Pasta, Rose and Tom, for the memories.

About the Author

Born on September 19, 1980 in Broadview Heights, Ohio to Frank Ng and Katherine Manzon. At the age of 2 ½, Vincent Yu-hin Ng began a 15 year journey with Suzuki Violin. Starting tennis in fourth grade, he won the Ohio State Championships as a sophomore in high school. One year later, he became the number one ranked player in the Midwest Section for Boys 18 and under. In 1997, Vincent won the National Gold Award for Pinhole Photography at the Corcoran Museum in Washington D.C. He was a "Lifer" at University School, graduating in 1999. After a 3 year tennis slump, he regained his form and won the 2001 U.S. National Amateur Hardcourt Championships. In 2003, he graduated the Ohio State University as the Big Ten Indoor Singles Champion and the Big Ten Player of the Year. He is the all-time winningest singles player at Ohio State. In his free time, he enjoys pursuing his latest hobby with his friends and having fun. He is currently attending Medical School at Ohio State and writing another book.

Works Cited

2001: A Space Odyssey Dir. Stanley Kubrick. Perf. Keir Dullea, Gary Lockwood. 1968.
Alcoholics Anonymous. "44 Questions." New York: Works Publishing, Inc. 1952.
Bonds, Barry. Interview with Peter Gammons. "Uncommon Bonds." ESPN the Magazine. New York. 14 Apr. 2003. p.69.
Bruch, Hilde. Don't be Afraid of your Child. New York: Farrar, Straus and Young, 1952. p.57.
Cape Fear. Dir. Martin Scorsese. Perf. Robert Deniro, Nick Nolte, Juliette Lewis. Universal Studios, 1991.
Coile, Caroline. Pit Bulls for Dummies. Indianapolis: Wiley Publishing, 2001.
Cooper, James Fenimore. The Last of the Mohicans. New York: Penguin Books, 1986. p.337, 339.
Cultic Studies: Information about Cults and Psychological Manipulation. 15 Mar 2004. http://csj.org/.
Emerson, Ralph W. The Portable Emerson. New York: Penguin Books, 1981. p.52-53.
Fischer, Bobby. 2 Aug. 2003. http://bobbfischer.net
Fitzgerald, F. Scott. The Great Gatsby. New York: Simon & Schuster, 1992. p.189.
Fraser, Tara. Total Yoga. USA: HarperCollins Publishers, 2001.
Goffman, Erving. The Presentation of Self in Everyday Life. New York: Doubleday, 1959. p.56.
Hesse, Hermann. Siddharta. New York: New Directions Publishing, 1951. p.111, 113.
Hesse, Hermann. Steppenwolf. New York: Henry Holt and Co., 1990. p.40.
*subtitle, *"Treatise on Tennis. Not for Everybody."* inspired by this book.
Hoffer, Eric. The True Believer: Thoughts on the Nature of Mass Movements. New York: HarperCollins Publishing, 2002.
Humphrey, Nicholas K., The Inner Eye. London: Faber and Faber, 1986.
Humphrey, Nicholas K., A History of the Mind. New York: HarperCollins, 1993.
Kingdom of Heaven Dir. Ridley Scott. Perf. Orlando Bloom, Liam Neeson, Jeremy Irons, Eva Green, Edward Norton. 2005
Koch Edward T., and Sandra DeSalvo. Complete Idiot's Guide to Investing Like a Pro. New York: Penguin Group, 1999.
Kolb, David. Learning Style Inventory. Boston: McBer and Company, 1985.
Lasch, Christopher. The Culture of Narcissism. New York: W. W. Norton and Co., 1979. p.53, 60, 64, 90.
A League of their Own. Dir. Penny Marshall. Perf. Tom Hanks, Madonna, Lori Petty. 1992.
Leakey, Richard. The Origin of Humankind. New York: Basic Books, 1996. [p.111-112?].
Lefton, Brad. "Ichiro Operates on a Higher Plane." Sporting News, May 15, 2005. http://msn.foxsports.com/mlb/story/3610314?GT1=6444
Leigh, Mitch, and Joe Darion. "Man of La Mancha." Perf. Peter O'Toole. New York: Broadway Musical, 1963.
London, Jack. The Call of the Wild & White Fang. New York: Fine Creative Media, 2003. p.231.
Lord of the Rings: The Fellowship of the Ring. Dir. Peter Jackson. Perf. Elijah Wood, Ian Mckellen. New Line Cinema, 2001.
MacYoung, Marc "The Animal," and Dianna Gorden. "Martial Arts Cults." 15 Jan 2004. http://www.nononsenseselfdefense.com/cults.htm.
Malamud, Bernard. The Natural. New York: Avon Books, 1952. p.26
"Maslow, Abraham." Bartlett's Familiar Quotations. 17th ed. 2002.

Mason, Robert, and Wanda Mason. "Mason's Opinions on Cults and Religious Abuse." 14 Mar 2004. http://www.gospelassemblyfree.com/facts.htm.
Miller, Arthur. Death of a Salesman. New York: Penguin Books, 1998. p.75.
Netter, Frank H. Atlas of Human Anatomy. 3rd ed. New Jersey, Icon Learning Systems, 2003.
Noonan, Peggy. "Why We Talk About Reagan." The Wall Street Journal.
Rainwater, Lee. Behind Ghetto Walls: Black Families in a Federal Slum. Chicago: Aldine, 1970. p.388-9.
Ring Generalship. 15 June 2003 http://stickgrappler.tripod.com/ug/rastushead.html
Searching for Bobby Fischer. Dir. Steven Zallian. Perf. Ben Kingsley, Joe Mantegna, Max Pomeranc. 1993.
Six Days, Seven Nights. Dir. Ivan Reitman. Perf. Harrison Ford, Anne Heche. Caravan Pictures, 1998.
Skelton, Paul. The Stafford Exchange. "Gameness, Aggression, and Prey Drive in Dogs." 15 June 2003. http://www.staffordmall.com/gamenessaggression.htm
Star Wars. Dir. George Lucas. Perf. Harrison Ford, James Earl Jones, Carrie Fisher. 1977.
Terminator 3: Rise of the Machines. Dir. Jonathan Mostow. Perf. Arnold Schwarzenegger. Warner Brothers, 2003.
Tolstoy, Leo. Anna Karenina. New York: Fine Creative Media, 2003. p.5.
Trading Places. Dir. John Landis. Perf. Dan Aykroyd, Eddie Murphy, Jamie Lee Curtis. Paramount Pictures, 1983.
Tressel, Jim. Coach Tressel's Pre-Game Speech Fiesta Bowl 2003. 31 Aug 2003. http://www.scottferguson.com/pages/TresselSpeech.html.
Walker, Texas Ranger. "Family Matters." Season 2, Episode 6. Perf. Chuck Norris. CBS, 20 Nov. 1993.
Waller, Willard. "The Rating and Dating Complex." American Sociological Review 2 1937, p.727-734.
Westlake, Doug. Essays on Martial Arts and Related Subjects. 15 June 2003. http://www.thewestcoast.net/gentlemengrapplers/essays.htm
Whitewater Reference. 25 July 2003. http://www.whitewatervoyages.com/reference/detailedglossary.html.
"Whatever It Takes: Pursuing the Perfect 10." CNN Presents rep. Carol Lin. CNN, 10 Aug. 2003.
Wolfenstein, Martha, and Nathan Leites. Movies: A Psychological Study. New York: Atheneum, 1970. p.31-33.
Wudka, Jose. Ockham's Razor. 24 Sep 1998. http://phyun5.ucr.edu/~wudka/physics7/notes_www/node10.htm.

Image Credits

Pg. 139. Bag Balm photo courtesy of the manufacturer.

> Dairy Association Co., Inc.
> PO Box 145
> Lyndonville, VT 05851
> 1-800-232-3610

Pg. 96. Forehand photo taken by Tim Revell, courtesy of The Columbus Dispatch.

Pg. 56. Low backhand photo taken by Mary Jo Walicki, courtesy of The Milwaukee Sentinel Journal

Pg. 64. Low forehand volley photo taken by Chris Parker, courtesy of The Southside Newspaper.

Final page photo of "The Violin Lesson" courtesy of The Cleveland Institute of Music.

All other photos taken by Katherine Manzon

All diagrams created by Vincent Ng

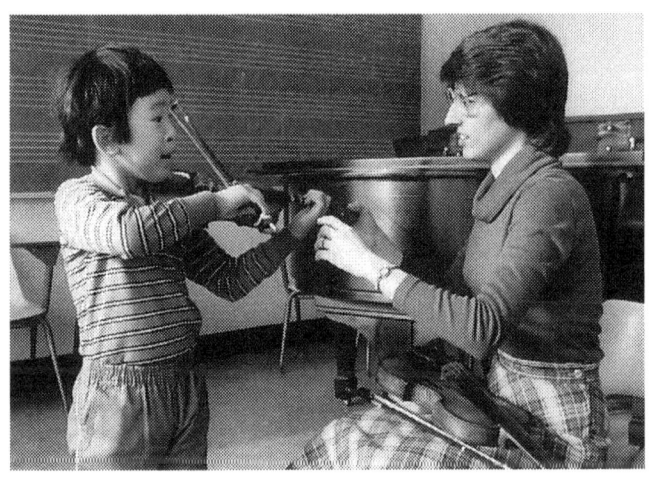

TODAY PUBLISHING

The Journey for Tomorrow Begins Today

www.ingramcontent.com/pod-product-compliance
Ingram Content Group UK Ltd.
Pitfield, Milton Keynes, MK11 3LW, UK
UKHW041418180426
11947UKWH00007B/196